Knocked Out But Not Down

Knocked Out But Not Down

One Bull Rider's Story of Faith and Resilience in the Aftermath of Multiple Concussions

Nick Morrison

Published by Life Sized Publishing

Oakville, Ontario, Canada

ISBN (paperback): 978-1-997730-19-4

ISBN (hardback): 978-1-997730-20-0

This book is dedicated to my wife, Ivy, and my two children, Tyler and Gracious. You three have ridden out this challenge with me, and I've never once heard any of you complain about it. You have always been there when I needed you and adapted on the fly when any situation arose. I would never have been able to survive this without you three.

Contents

Foreword

by W. Russell Merck

Serendipity: a happy, unexpected discovery – finding something good or useful by chance.

It was a chance meeting. I had endured a two-day conference that sapped my energy and drained the last drops of my strength. I just wanted it to end so I could go home. I was prepared to sprint for the door as soon as the closing speaker spoke his last words. It was only he who stood between me and the freedom for which my heart desperately yearned.

After a brief introduction, a tall man in his early 40s, wearing jeans, a long-sleeve western shirt, and a cowboy hat, approached the lectern. My mind screamed, "What!?!?! This conference has nothing to do with cowboys, horses, or tumbleweeds. Why on earth would they choose to close with a cowboy?" It turns out he was a stand-up comic who had been hired to tell us how he single-handedly, and highly successfully, booked himself at dance halls and music venues all across the nation. This was indeed an appropriate topic for our group of talent booking agents from across the state of Texas. And he was a comedian. I thought, "Well, at least I'll have a few laughs before I leave."

My internal dialogue fell silent when he began to speak. He had a powerful, confident voice. He was poised and professional. This cowboy looked like he had been speaking in front of audiences for years (he had). You've guessed by now, his name was Nick Morrison.

His informal, conversational style made him incredibly easy to listen to. I soon learned that in addition to being a cowboy, he was a master storyteller. Without realizing it, my thoughts of getting to the door vanished. I was now on the edge of my seat, hanging on every word, riveted by this cowboy and his story.

Nick had suffered multiple concussions during his career as a professional bull rider. His many concussions led to a lifetime of challenges, many of which he still faces daily. Yet, when you meet him, he comes across as an unassuming, modest cowboy. I can tell you; he is that and much more. Serendipity brought us together that day. I owe serendipity a debt of gratitude. Knowing Nick Morrison has created significant and lasting change in my life. He is not only a successful bull rider, but also a man of faith who lives by simple but enduring principles: honesty, integrity, dedication to family, hard work, and friendship, to name a few. I feel fortunate and proud to call him "friend."

After he finished his talk that day, rather than sprinting for the door, I stayed to thank him for the great inspiration he had given me. I waited for other well-wishers to shake his hand and say thank you. I finally had my chance to attempt to communicate what his story meant to me. I told him that because of his story and his speaking ability, he had the makings of an incredible inspirational speech. I have now retired, but had the tremendous good fortune to spend my career as a professional speaker, traveling throughout the U.S. and many other countries delivering messages of hope and encouragement. As I spoke to him, I began to have a feeling there was something special about this man. I think it was a combination of his humble demeanor, his incredible story, and his unassuming nature that gave me a deep belief that this message needed to be shared with others, many others.

Nick told me he had begun writing a book about his life and the many adversities he has had to overcome. But he had put it aside due to his busy life as a comedian, father, and husband. I beseeched him to continue the book project; the world needed to hear his story. A few months later, Nick found Life Sized Publishing. They, too, thought his story was inspiring, so inspiring that they offered him a publishing contract. What emerged was something I would never have expected.

This cowboy, who was an incredible speaker with an amazing life story, was also an outstanding writer. I'm a tough audience. I've read lots of books, even written two myself. I don't believe I am overstating things when I say *Knocked Out But Not Down* is among the best books I have ever read. The same conversational style and master storytelling that made his speaking so engaging are reflected directly in his writing. This book is at the same time, funny, inspiring, and incredibly well written. Each sentence flows seamlessly into the next. His detailed, unhurried storytelling creates vivid images that jump off the page. This book is as easy and enjoyable to read as it is inspirational and life changing.

Whether you want to avoid concussions, suffer from the aftermath of concussions, or are facing some other adversity in your life, I know *Knocked Out But Not Down* will provide the inspiration you need to overcome any challenge. It will help you reach beyond overcoming adversity. It will teach you how to thrive in the face of it.

– *W. Russell Merck*

International Speaker/Author/Consultant

Note from the Author

Thank you very much for taking the time to read this book. I poured everything I had into writing it and relived some very difficult emotions to ensure the whole story was told.

I chose the title *Knocked Out But Not Down* because it not only resonated with the amount of times I've literally been knocked out in my life, but also because of what that term means to me when it is phrased in that order. Most hear that phrase and think it should be switched with "knocked down but not out," meaning "You may have knocked me down, but I'm still in this fight." And that's great. But what about the times in life that blind-side you to the point of sending your entire world around you into a tailspin? Anytime you're sticking your chin out in life, taking risks to succeed, all it takes is one perfectly located punch to derail everything. The best boxers in the world can train and be prepared as much as possible for their fight, but one well placed punch, and that boxer now finds himself lying on the mat – knocked out. What do you do when you've been hit so hard with an adversity you didn't see coming, that the world is now spinning out of control around you? When you are lying on the mat disoriented, in shock, and trying to comprehend what just happened; *that* is when the true inner fight begins. Your mind and entire body are telling you that it's okay to stop. Stay down. Live to fight another day. Accept defeat. It takes true resilience to not only stand back up, but to stand back up ready to fight stronger than you were before. Life may have knocked me out multiple times, but it won't keep me down.

Even though concussions ended up being the focal point, by default, I tried to add something in here for everyone. Inspiration, entertainment, motivation, education, and awareness were the five objectives I wanted to instill throughout the entire writing process.

This book is riddled with stories – some entertaining, some serious. My goal was to take a fiction writer's approach to real-life stories that truly happened, as wild as they may seem, and paint a picture in a way where you, the reader, feel as if you were there living through the stories with me.

The one feedback from beta readers that has resonated the most with me is how they felt a rollercoaster of emotions from cover to cover. That's how I felt living through it – extreme highs and extreme lows. I don't want to paint myself as more than I am and remain humbled that you would take the time to read what I have to say.

I hope this book fills you with *all* of the emotions at some point. I hope it makes you laugh, makes you think, makes you reflect, and possibly even makes you cry – I know it did me while reliving certain events. I hope it educates you on concussions, concussion issues, rodeo, and maybe even yourself. I hope there is something you can take away from this book that helps you; may it be with someone dealing with concussions in your life or your own difficulties and adversities you are facing.

Most importantly, I want to express my utmost gratitude to you, the reader. Thank you for investing yourself and your time into the next 18 chapters as I expose my story, my struggles, my adversities, and my victories.

– *Nick Morrison*

Chapter 1

Why Write This Book?

The Morrison kids dressed for church circa 1985 Nate (5), Tammy (9), and Nick (3) Photo courtesy of Mary Scott

Take care of concussions.

If you are around me long enough you will eventually hear me say that phrase. Sometimes I say it as a punch-line to a joke making fun of myself. Other times I say it in all seriousness because someone just witnessed me pass out and fall face-first to the floor for no apparent reason at all. But the reality is: take care of concussions.

The big question I have to answer, before opening my life up to you in an extremely vulnerable level of transparency, is "*Why write this book?*" I've been knocked out more times than I can count, but I've never let myself be knocked down to the point of quitting. As the title of the book explains, I've been *Knocked Out But Not Down*. Faced with numerous career changes and multiple "life resets," I have learned to look forward to the next challenge rather than focusing backwards on "what could have been." I can also bring a unique aspect to the subject of concussions that most can't articulate. The very essence of my heart is to help and to bless people. So, if that means opening myself up in ways beyond my comfort zone, then so be it.

I will be using a lot of rodeo or cowboy terminology throughout this book. To keep from stopping the flow of the book to explain these, I have added a section to the back of the book that you can use as a reference as you read. That section will define these terms, give some background as to why those terms are used, and even give some behind-the-scenes insight into rodeo through those terms. If you read a term you are not familiar with, check this section as it may be defined there. I encourage you to utilize this tool as you read, as it may help you understand the sport of rodeo more as well. I will even add a few extra rodeo terms not used in this book to give a wider spectrum of the sport.

The purpose of this book is three-fold. I have been public speaking in some form or fashion since I was 15 years old. Something I hear often is, "We love your stories, Nick! You need to put some of your stories into a book." So this book will be very story-driven. Stories will be the anchor that facilitates the other two main purposes of this book.

The second purpose is to encourage, inspire, and motivate others to conquer whatever adversity they may be facing. Throughout my life, as you will learn, I have had to push through *layers* of adversity. Dreams crushed. Careers ended. House destroyed by a hurricane. Having to teach myself how to speak again. And those are just skimming the surface. I have watched my brother overcome something even harder, seeing his rodeo career end with a broken neck that left him paralyzed from the armpits down. So, my hope is to use my stories, and parts of my brother's story, to show you it is possible to be successful despite adversities, to encourage you to face your difficulties head-on and come out victorious on the other side.

The third goal of this book is the most important of the three to me personally: to help those who struggle with concussion issues. I want to put you into the mindset of somebody who has had dozens of concussions, and who had to learn to fight through complications *daily* as a result. I want you to understand that multiple concussions during a short period of time can have lifelong repercussions. I want to emphasize the importance of preventing concussions and seeking early medical care if a concussion does occur.

Maybe you are reading this book because you have a child who has had a concussion and you are looking deeper into its effect. Maybe you are reading this because you yourself deal with the repercussions from a series of concussions. Maybe you are simply reading this book because someone heard you had a concussion at some point in your life, so they put this book in your hands. You told them you would read it knowing all too well you don't read books. Then after the book sat on a shelf for a few months you needed some "reading material" because your phone battery died, and you knew you were going to be in the bathroom for a while. So … here we are.

Regardless of your reasoning, you are reading this book. While my hope is that my stories entertain you; even more, I hope this book helps you. I hope it helps shed some light on the seriousness of letting concussions stack on top of each other. If you are someone who has dealt with concussions, I hope it helps you get a grip on the reality of the side effects they cause and maybe gives you a slight advantage in dealing with them from now on. If you know someone who has had concussions, then I hope this book helps you to understand them better. If you are a spouse of someone with concussion problems then I hope this book helps you become the support system your spouse needs, and that you realize they can't survive this without you.

The truth is I don't wish my life on anybody. I don't even wish it upon my worst enemy; to feel the way I feel daily or to have to deal with the struggles I deal with. It took me a long time to realize that for me to fully help myself, I had to let others know what I was dealing with. I knew they probably wouldn't understand any of it or be able to wrap their mind around my struggles, but my story needed to be shared. The more I told my story, the more I realized that I was not alone. I learned that my own friends – people I've spent a lot of time around – are dealing with similar issues; something I had no idea of because they were just as hesitant to talk about it as I used to be. We became a support group for each other because, unless you live it, you truly can't understand it. After praying about it, I have decided to put my story on paper to hopefully help somebody else who needs it.

This is not a medical book. I am many things – a former bull rider, storyteller, musician, motivational speaker, writer, stand-up comedian – but I am not a doctor. I am simply someone who is living with the after-effects of multiple concussions. While I will try my hardest to be as medically accurate as possible, post-concussion syndrome manifests differently in each person. What you will get in this book is my experiences. My stories.

My name is Nick Morrison.

I am a husband, a father, a son, and a brother. I am a normal person, though some may argue that fact with you, who has had too many concussions to count and now struggles with the effects of brain damage every day.

I was raised on a ranch on the Pine Ridge Indian Reservation in Potato Creek, South Dakota. With the *Dances With Wolves* scenery as my backdrop I grew up with a true cowboy lifestyle. We raised Black Angus cattle for beef, as well as bucking horses and bucking bulls to be used in the sport of rodeo. I lived on the back of a horse in wide-open pastures as far as the eye could see in every direction. Many would call my childhood their dream lifestyle. I didn't know anything else. To me living almost 100 miles away from our shopping, 50 miles from my school, 50 miles from the closest bank or post office, and over 20 miles away from my hometown of less than a hundred people was normal. All I knew was we woke up before sunrise, saddled our horses, and went to work.

Rodeo is a way of life where I come from. It's not a simple high school sport or a part-time hobby. Rodeo was my dream. It was all my friends' dreams. In most states, like Texas where I live now, the 'Friday Night Lights' of high school football take center stage. In South Dakota, rodeo reigns supreme! It's something kids start when they are young and continue as long as they can. To see a World Champion Rodeo Athlete at the local sale barn isn't that big of a deal. Why? Because we all grew up together. We went to school together. We talked about the "rodeo dream" together.

Almost every town in western South Dakota, no matter how big or small, has a rodeo arena. Small towns explode in population whenever a rodeo is in town, even if it's only an amateur event. Rodeo really is that popular of a sport in that region. The festivities of a rodeo benefit the economy of the entire community. Many rodeos become a celebration for the whole county; with parades during the day and live-music street dances at night. Business owners see a spike in revenue while local ranchers see an opportunity to have an entertaining break from their normal day-to-day grind at the ranch.

So, of course. I jumped into rodeo life with both feet. After living in Wyoming – where I was born on a large family ranch that has been in our family for over a century – and following short stints in Montana, North Dakota, and Oklahoma, my family and I moved to South Dakota when I was 10 years old. My dad took over pastoring a church on the Pine Ridge Indian Reservation. I caught the bug and started riding steers within the first year of moving there – when the newly crowned World Champion bull rider, Cody Custer, came to our house to do a bull riding clinic in 1993. By the time I was 12, I was riding bulls. By 16, it had become a full-time pursuit of a dream.

Most cowboys in our area eventually become saddle bronc riders – and some of the best in the world, I might add – but not me. I loved riding bulls too much. I loved the thrill and the adrenaline rush. I loved the fact that a Barney Fife look-a-like as myself could strap his hand into a bull rope and immediately feel like another more famous Morrison: John Wayne. Besides that, I was good at it. I could actually make a living doing something I loved. It wasn't a hobby to me. It was a passion, a calling, and a way of life.

Bull riding is considered a contact sport. I guess you could say that over the course of my career, I got contacted. My entire professional career was spent almost exclusively injured with one frustration after another. Every time I recovered from one injury and gained momentum, I would end up back on the couch rehabbing once again. Injuries are to be expected with all contact sports, especially bull riding. A few years ago, the *Journal of the San Francisco Medical Society* published a report stating that the injury rate for bull riding is 10.3 times the injury rate for American football.[1] At times, it

1. Martínez, A, et al. "Bull Riding Is More Dangerous than Football.

felt like I had 10.3 times more injuries than my fellow bull riders.

I battled multiple broken ribs, a broken tailbone twice, a cracked C-2 vertebra in my neck, broken T-10 and T-11 vertebrae in my back, torn groin muscles, multiple broken or dislocated fingers, dislocated both shoulders numerous times, a dislocated knee, and a separated shoulder, just to name a few. Of all my broken bones and torn-up joints — including my career-ending injury when I was only 21 years old — the injuries that have affected me the most over the long term are the ones that seemed like nothing at the time: my concussions.

During the final six-year period of my bull riding career – spanning from the ages of 16 to 21 – it is calculated that I had more than 20 recorded concussions. Most likely, I experienced many more. We truly don't know how many more concussions I have incurred, but if I add just the number of times I've been knocked out since then – by playing too rough with my dogs, doing something idiotic to tickle my need to feel adrenaline, or simply by passing out and hitting my head while bouncing off an object on the way to the ground – we stopped counting at 50 total.

Head injuries are fickle things. With each concussion, it became easier to get a new one. A concussion isn't

---

Here's Why Two Teenagers Love It." NPR, NPR, 1 Nov. 2024, www.npr.org/2024/09/27/nx-s1-5129717/nevada-teenage-cowboys-rodeo.

incurred by a blow to the outside of the head like most people think. A concussion happens when the brain moves rapidly inside the skull; especially if the brain slaps up against the cranium. The more concussions a person gets without letting the brain fully heal, the more "loose" their brain gets inside their skull. It feels, anymore, that if I sneeze too hard, I get another one. In fact, just a few days ago, I sneezed so hard I knocked myself out again. My wife said I was just sitting on the couch, sneezed violently, slumped over, and then my arms went completely stiff; a telltale sign I've been knocked out.

When I experienced the majority of my concussions, it seemed every doctor had a different treatment plan. "Don't fall asleep for at least 12 hours." "You need to sleep this off immediately." "Ahh, it's just a bump to the head, you'll be fine." I am glad to see that the medical community has learned more about concussion treatment in recent years, and that the sports community is taking concussions more seriously as a result.

The reality is, though, we truly don't know every detail about concussions. I don't think we ever will. But concussions are being looked at more now than ever, as they should be. I am living proof of the side effects that multiple concussions can bring and I don't wish it upon anyone.

I now constantly live with that feeling you get after you have a severe concussion. I'm always nauseous. I'm always irritable. Any bright lights give me an instant headache, many times a severe migraine. Whenever I take the stage, as a comedian or motivational speaker, I am fighting through a headache the entire time I'm up there due to the bright lights shining in my face. If I throw up in the Green Room bathroom when I walk off stage, it's not because of nerves but because I laid it all out on the line for the crowd in attendance, and the migraine from the bright lights finally caught up with me.

I get car sick extremely easily now. When I puke from car sickness, it's never pretty either. It's violent. I have to either be driving or in the front-passenger seat or else instantaneous car-sickness hits, especially if I get hot inside the car. Even that doesn't always prevent it, though. My Relief Band has been the best purchase I've ever made as it has helped lessen the motion-sickness occurrences since wearing it.

I am in a constant state of light-headedness that makes it always feel like I am standing on a plywood sheet floating over an air hockey table. Those symptoms never go away. I don't experience side effects from Benadryl because how people explain what they feel after taking a couple of those pills is a small part of how I already feel 24/7.

The hardest to ride-out is when I get this feeling that can only be described as "claustrophobic in my own skin." I just want to tear my skin off as every inch of my body tingles with heat, seemingly squeezing the air out of me, and I can't escape the feeling no matter how hard I try.

But those are just the tip of the iceberg of what I deal with – and my wife deals with – on a daily basis. If I look straight up to the sky, chances are I will pass out. If I bend over to pick something up, chances are I will pass out. If I look too quickly from one direction to the other, spin in a circle, or let my heart rate get too high, chances are, you guessed it, I will pass out. As you can tell, I pass out a lot. It has earned me the nickname EffGee among my closest friends; which stands for FG, which in turn stands for their own personal Fainting Goat.

Usually when I pass out, it isn't very graceful either. I'll bounce off every object in my way on my path to the ground. I feel like my wife is a schoolyard nurse with as many rug burns, cuts, and scrapes she is always doctoring on my body after the many times I have scraped across the carpet during an epic wipe-out.

That's not even dipping into the sensory and memory issues. It took me a long time to realize most of these were tied to my concussions. For instance, I drop things a lot. Out of nowhere my hand will inexplicably decide it doesn't want to grip anymore, and now I have broken glass and chocolate milkshake all over my floor.

I can't remember the last time I didn't have a loud ringing or chirping sound in my ears. Most of the time, I can block it out like an annoying mosquito. But there are times it will elevate into an ear-splitting pitch that is too loud to ignore. It can be triggered by a loud "bang" noise or simply come out of the blue. If I am in conversation with someone when one starts, I will read their lips to follow in the conversation so they won't catch on that I can't hear a word they are saying. In the worst cases it brings me to my knees in pain as the entire world spins out-of-control around me.

I don't remember people; people I should remember. It's an embarrassing feeling of having a full conversation with someone — either from my past or a current acquaintance — and I can't figure out who they are. We are talking together, but the whole time I am faking the conversation while having a whole other conversation in my head. "*They look familiar so surely I know 'em. They are talking to me like we're good friends. Why can't I place them? Did I hear someone call him George? He looks like a George. But what if George isn't his name? Then if I call him George, he will realize I don't remember who he is, and he is going to get offended because he won't understand. This could get messy. I will just call him 'Bud'.*"

I've learned to call many people "Bud". That way if I forget who they are, they won't know the difference. I realize now that people I've been calling "Bud" for years may read this book and are going to have that awkward realization that I may not actually remember their name. Oh well. That's a risk I'm going to have to take.

My wife, Ivy, is amazing and can tell that "look" in my eyes that nobody else can; that lost look my eyes portray when my brain is going 100 mph behind the scenes trying to decipher everything. She will lean into my ear and whisper, "His name is Tom. You guys went fishing together a few weeks ago. He has a wife named Julie and a son named Jack."

Good thing I didn't call him George. I then proceed to have an entire conversation with Tom until it starts to slowly come back to me who he is and how I know him.

A few years ago I was standing with my brother — well, I was standing anyway — at the South Point in Las Vegas a couple nights before the NFR (National Finals Rodeo) started. The South Point Resort and Casino, on the days leading up to the NFR, is like a reunion party every night of rodeo athletes and stock contractors, new and old. Every stock contractor in the building seemed to line up to have a conversation with my brother. He is now one of the world's leading brokers, through his business, The Breeders Connection, for the sale of bucking stock between producers, contractors, people who want to get into the business, and people who simply want to invest in bucking bulls as partners.

While my brother was talking to someone else, a man walked up to me all excited and said, "Man, I haven't seen you in forever!" while giving me a big hug. I didn't have the slightest clue who this guy was. He started the whole "Do remember when?" stories and I did the fake "Oh ya! Ya, ya, ya, ya, ya. You tell the story though, because you tell it better" still oblivious to this person's identity or any of the stories he was telling. After about a 20-minute conversation, he walked away and I had to ask my brother who that was. He seemed shocked and answered, "That was your traveling partner for, like, two years."

For those who have never been around rodeo, you need to understand how important traveling partners are. They would be the equivalent of teammates in other sports. These are the guys we spend that season with going up and down the road. We see them more than our families. We spend tens of thousands of miles in the car together. We do everything with them. They are our best friends. So you can imagine how horrible I felt that I didn't recognize someone who was that close to me at one point in my life. I used to pride myself in being able to remember not only everyone I met, but something interesting about them as well to bring back up in a conversation if I ever met them again. Of all the annoyances that come with my issues, this is the one that bothers me the most.

I don't remember many things from my past. I have become very "story driven." The main reason is because without telling these stories over and over again, I am afraid of what little I will remember. Sometimes I will find my brain melding multiple instances into one occurrence. Some of these stories in this book may have happened over time, but how I remember them is how I am telling them. Someone who was there may remember the story happening differently than I do, and, let's be honest, their version is probably the more accurately remembered one. I had so many concussions during my college years that the entire college-period of my life is one big blur. Many people may say the same thing about their college years, but their "college blur" is probably because of a completely different reasoning than mine.

One of the greatest feelings for me, now, is when I see something that triggers an old memory. Once I get that nugget of the old memory, it starts to unlock more. I find myself filled with excitement as memories of the past start to flood back, one after the other.

The worst feeling is when I all of a sudden don't recognize where I am and even sometimes who I am. It is like everything over the last few hours never existed and nothing around me looks familiar. When this happens, I will simply sit back and observe or read as many things around me as I can to try to piece together my scenario until I can get a grip on where I am and what is going on. Sometimes this works. Sometimes it doesn't. Like when it happened to me in Germany. I tried to read the words on the signs around me – in my mind, I assumed I was in America – only to come to the realization "*I have also forgotten how to read!!*"

I have learned little things to combat this. From writing my name in places where I know, from past experiences, I will typically look first; to understanding my parameters of when I may be pushing myself too hard to make this possibly happen again. Sometimes it isn't a bad "brain episode," as my wife and I have started calling it, and I can piece things together before anyone even knows it happened.

Other times my wife has to come find me based on the vague descriptions I am giving her over the phone. Or, like an incident from a few years ago, where I didn't recognize my own house and, for some reason, just took off walking, thinking I would figure out where I was eventually. Then I kind of "jumped forward in time" and, all of a sudden, realized I was in some stranger's car because he found me walking two miles from my house. "*I feel like I should know him based on how he is talking to me and how he knows where I live. Maybe his name is George, I don't know.*" On a side note, if you are the man who picked me up two miles from my home one day and drove me back, please tell us who you are because we have *not* been able to figure it out yet. Maybe it is one of those instances the Bible talks about where we will entertain angels without even knowing it.

This may all seem shocking to you. I may even have close friends read this book and say, "Wow, I never knew." That's because I am married to the most amazing person ever. She protects me. She took college courses on brain injuries just so she could understand me better. She knows how embarrassing it is for me to have these things happen. The only reason I am telling my story now is because I realize there are others like me out there. Maybe by reading my story, it will help them understand their issues better as well.

As dark as these side effects may seem, the reality is that there is an even darker side to concussions – one nobody, until recently, wanted to even talk about. But it is also a reality that most people don't understand how these dark episodes are tied to their concussions. It is still difficult for me to talk about it, but I also know it is crucial to tell the *whole* story. So as hard as this subject is, we are going to tackle it head-on in this book.

I am fortunate that I have been able to use what I have learned, through my many struggles with concussion issues, to inspire others through their problems as well. What I *get* to do for a living now feels like a dream to me. While I love touring the United States as a stand-up comedian, even more I love being able to inspire others as a motivational speaker. Over the years I have been very blessed to travel all over the world speaking into the lives of many people. Companies, organizations, conferences, conventions, churches, and schools have brought me in to encourage their crowds. Inspiring others is a huge part of what makes my heart beat, and what makes me work so hard every morning to still function at a level where I can continue to bless others. Therefore, you will see a lot of the "motivational" side of me come out periodically in this book.

Until recently I didn't speak of my concussion issues from the stage. Once I started opening up about them, I realized the impact telling my story could have on helping others. Whether it is speaking to a few dozen real estate agents at a regional gathering, inspiring a school assembly full of our next generation, or motivating a crowd of thousands at a convention or conference; I will always have at least one person come up and share their story, or a family member's story, of how concussions have impacted their life.

One recurring theme I hear, when long-term effects come into the conversation, is the phrase "We hid the concussions from..." Maybe it's a coach, a trainer, a family member; whoever it is, they felt the need to hide that concussion so that they, or their child, could continue to compete. I hope my story helps convey the importance of letting a concussion heal *fully*. Getting to see your child compete that weekend isn't worth what that child could face as an adult if the concussion is ignored.

While I hope my stories entertain some of you, my true hope for this book is that it helps someone. This is not the "know all" book for concussions or overcoming adversity. This is simply my story, my struggles, my experiences, and how I have learned to combat life as a result.

In this book, I will take you through the timeline of my concussion issues. I will take you into my mind and thought process through each stage as well. My main hope is to bring you along through the roller coaster of emotions I felt and understand what was going through my mind at that time. My goal is to help you understand the thought process of a loved one who may be dealing with the same issues, or to help you cope with the issues or thoughts you may be facing yourself. If just one person can read my story and it helps them piece their own puzzle together, or it helps them overcome their own concussion issues, then all of the work that went into this book was worth it to me.

So with that, let's begin.

Chapter 2

Childhood as an Adrenaline Junkie

Brothers Nate (7) on Buster and Nick Morrison (4) on Cinnamon riding out with their dad to check cows one morning in 1987 Photo courtesy of Mary Scott

"*If I didn't fall off my horse from laughing at you, then it wasn't a good enough wreck.*"

That was the lifestyle I grew up around. It was never boring. There was always something to entertain us. If there wasn't then we made our own entertainment. If somebody wasn't getting hurt then we evidently weren't making it entertaining enough. Combine that with our need to fill our adrenaline addiction and this may be a big factor as to why my brother was paralyzed at 18 years old and why, five years later, my bull riding career was over at only 21 years old.

Adrenaline is a funny thing. At its core, adrenaline is designed to keep us safe. It gives us that extra boost we need to fight or flee potentially scary situations. But once your body experiences a large rush of adrenaline, it can become highly addictive. Bull riding is a perfect example. I can merely *attempt* to describe to you the intoxicating feeling a person has when riding a bull, and I still won't be able to do it justice. Everything slows down. You feel invincible. It becomes a chess match between you and this extremely intelligent, far-stronger animal underneath you. The countless hours of groundwork to train your muscle memory finally pay off as your body makes the necessary moves before you can even "think" to make them. No matter if it is in the practice pen or in front of a crowd of tens of thousands of people, you hear this tunnel of silence brought on by your intense concentration in the moment. The higher caliber the bull, or event, the more extreme this feeling becomes. Then there is that moment when a crowd is large enough, and your ride is good enough, that the sheer volume of the crowd cheering breaks your internal silence. It is one of the greatest feelings in the world.

The adrenaline rush a person gets when riding a bull, no matter the caliber of bull, is unmatched. In fact, many people's memory will "black out" the first few bulls they get on. This isn't a reaction of fear. This is a reaction to the body being overloaded with more adrenaline than it is accustomed to. As a result, the mind simply cannot recall what just happened. As the body begins to adapt to this adrenaline rush, that person typically remembers more from their rides as they progress. If someone has been riding long enough, eventually they will get to a point in their high school or amateur days where they will get tapped-off on a bloop spinner and their mind wanders mid-ride to what kind of toppings they want to put on their pizza after the rodeo at the local pizza parlor they passed on the drive there. Even the best bull riders in the world, though, will tell you that when they get to that "elite level," it will still take them a few minutes to recall portions of many of their rides, if they ever do recall them. At that level, the adrenaline rush is unrivaled.

But here is where the normal life of a bull rider starts to change, especially if they have experienced these high levels of adrenaline since childhood. The things that are considered fun and entertaining for everyone else are now extremely boring. Simply sledding with friends as kids is no longer fun. They start to come up with ways to sled that could seriously hurt somebody because it's the only way to get enough adrenaline to make it less boring. I am not knocking adrenaline or adrenaline-junkies one bit! I am one! I just want you to understand the mindset behind many of the things we did on our ranch growing up.

If social media and online video outlets would have been around when my brother and I were kids, we would have been internet sensations. We didn't simply do fun things. We. Had. Fun. We had a playground of thousands of acres, many steep hills, and a hillside of broken-down farm machinery, old wagons, and other farm-auction delights at our fingertips. Our dad taught us to weld at a very young age. This meant we could use that scrap to build anything our minds dreamed up. His rule was, "As long as there is sunlight, you can't be inside. If you are bored, I always have fence that needs fixin'." Our ranch had miles upon miles of wooden posts and barbed wire fencing that always needed tended to. We hated fixing fence. I would be happy if I never saw another spool of barbed wire, post-hole diggers, or wire stretchers another day in my life. So we would do anything we could to stay busy if it meant it kept us from fixing fences.

I can't even remember 90% of the death traps my brother and I built. It's a miracle we are both alive, to be honest with you. But we wanted to have fun, and to have fun, we had to match the adrenaline we were getting on the weekends. This is why I was only given one bicycle over the entirety of my childhood.

For my 10th birthday, I finally received a bicycle I had always wanted. Where most kids are content with riding their bikes around in circles, I was not. Within two hours, that bike was totaled after I came screaming down the hill on the driveway leading to our house, realized I didn't know how to brake, and slammed the bike full-speed into the log fence surrounding the front yard; flipping over the fence and into my mom's flowerbed on the other side. But do not be dismayed. As my brother and I used to quote from our favorite show, *The Red Green Show*: "If the women can't find you handsome, they can at least find you handy." We fixed that bike right up and were back to riding it before the week was over. But once again, simply riding it up and down hills was no longer fun. We had to find the steepest hill with a drop-off at the end into a small patch of grass leading to a grove of pine trees.

Riding down the hill and off the drop-off was fun for about an hour. Now what can we do to make it more fun and more dangerous? Let's build a jump/ramp at the bottom of the hill and the top of the drop-off! That sounds completely legit! So for the rest of the day, we built our ramp. All it took was one pass. No trial runs. No sitting down drawing mathematical equations in the dirt or understanding the scientific physics behind our hair-brained schemes. Nope. One run right out of the gate, and we would know if it would work or not. It did, indeed, *not* work. Maybe we should have drawn *some* mathematical equations in the sand. We highly underestimated that the distance my brother would travel in the air and the distance from the ramp to the trees would intersect with each other. In one run, I now had an older brother tangled up in trees with a scraped-up body from head to toe, a bike with the front wheel bent at a 90-degree angle, the seat bent to the handlebars, and the chain snapped in two. But boy, was it fun for those few seconds! Once I got done rolling on the ground laughing at my brother, I assisted him out of his predicament in the trees.

This wasn't something new for us either. This was every day; even back when we were little kids. Like when we were five and seven years old, had just watched the movie *Ben Hur* with our parents, and now wanted to be chariot racers. Saddling our miniature pony, Cinnamon, then tying one end of a rope to the saddle horn and the other end of the rope to our tricycle seemed like a fully legitimate thing a chariot racer would do, at least in the minds of a couple of kids. Luckily for us, the pony spooked before either of us could mount our chariot. Watching the tricycle bounce back and forth, upside down, right side up, hitting every tree it could find in its path as Cinnamon was in full-runaway mode, we now realized the error in our judgment. This was ranch life. It is definitely not for the faint of heart.

Fast forward to my freshman year in high school. We were traveling to a series of high school rodeos over three days scattered hundreds of miles apart. A large group of us bull riders, bareback riders, and saddle bronc riders always traveled together and stayed at each other's houses; whichever was closest to the next event. In this case, around 15 of us were staying at a friend's farm. Imagine 15 high school-age boys, all adrenaline junkies, staying together. This is where things would get fun, or dangerous, depending on how you would perceive it if you were our fathers or our mothers.

Our friend had taken a motorcycle-racing engine and installed it into his go-cart. Then he welded roll bars around the outside. He hadn't had a chance to try his new death contraption yet. So, naturally all us boys decided we would have some fun and give it a spin in the dark that night. Our friend wasn't necessarily a math genius and didn't make any measurements whatsoever. He just welded what looked good. When we went to get inside the go-kart, we realized his most glaring mistake: there was only enough room inside the roll bars to fit one small person. My friend, Jason Stuen, was the only person small enough to fit, so he got to be the only person to drive the souped-up go-kart. As you can tell, this wasn't fun for any of us but him. We had to find a way to make this fun for all of us.

Why not bring a 4-wheeler into the equation? If we could get enough speed with the 4-wheeler, and the go-kart had enough steam going itself, we could ram Jason in the go-kart with the 4-wheeler and make him roll like a pecan being tossed across the room. This was a blast! I can still, to this day, hear Jason's laughter from inside the protective roll cage! But there was another problem. Now only one person at a time got to ram into Jason. So what would any group of teenage boys looking for an adrenaline rush do in this situation? We crammed as many people onto the 4-wheeler as we could. If you are curious how many teenagers one can cram onto a 4-wheeler, eight at a time is as good of a number as we could come up with. This sounds highly dangerous and unsafe to you? That's because it was. Looking back, it was plain idiotic. But at the time, it was fun. Up until everything turned south.

Picture this. I was sitting on the back left corner of the 4-wheeler. My feet were dangling off the side with the sidewall of the back left wheel directly behind my calves and feet. I had only half of my butt-cheek on the 4-wheeler. The other half couldn't fit because, as I stated earlier, there were eight of us on that one tiny machine. I was hanging onto the back rack with both hands as tightly as I could. We were flying across the pasture trying to ram Jason harder than we did the previous time, when I got an annoying itch on my nose. I hung on tight with one hand and let go with the other so I could scratch the itch.

At that moment, the left side of the 4-wheeler hit a big hole. It bounced the 4-wheeler halfway in the air and shot me off of the back like a cannon. I don't remember anything after that moment, but according to my friends, I made about 1 1/2 head-over-heels rotations before crashing back to the ground. I was knocked out cold. My friends thought they killed me. After a few minutes, I finally came to. Things were cloudy. My whole body ached. But nothing was broken and I came out unscathed. Or so I thought.

This was my first major concussion. While things seemed slightly out of the ordinary at the time, looking back, it really seemed like nothing in comparison to other concussions later in my life. But all concussion issues have to start somewhere. And mine started that day on a small farm outside of Murdo, South Dakota.

Chapter 3

When a Helmet Saved My Life

Nick (16) on Broken Leg of Bierema Rodeo Company "Riding for Nate" one year after his brother, Nate, broke his neck in the same arena, leaving him paralyzed from the chest down. Photo courtesy of Plooster Photography

SOME KIDS WANT A SWIMMING POOL IN THEIR BACKYARD. Others want an immaculate tree house. My brother and I wanted our own arena with bucking chutes, so that's exactly what our dad built for us. This was great because we could practice riding bulls or bucking horses any time we wanted. Our friends drove from hundreds of miles away to stay with us just so they could practice too. My dad used it as a ministry tool. He didn't charge people money to practice, like most places available for practice did back then. Instead, for every bull or horse a person got on at our house, that person owed my dad one church service somewhere down the road. Between the hundreds of miles he drives throughout the week – to places in South Dakota and Nebraska to have weekly church services for those in remote rural areas – and all of the church services we did at rodeos every weekend, they had plenty of opportunities to "pay up" for getting on as many horses or bulls as their heart desired. Many future stars in the Professional Rodeo world, whether as contestants or stock contractors, spent their childhood and high school days with us in that arena.

Our neighbors always had this fear that if one of their breed bulls jumped the fence and got into one of our pastures, my brother and I would gather them to the house, run them in the chute, and try to ride them. They probably had that fear because it was exactly what we would do. It was a good deterrent, though, because they were more motivated to keep their fences fixed. Either that or they would be in a bigger hurry to come gather one of their bulls who hopped into one of our pastures.

Most bucking bulls are bred to buck through their bloodlines. Breed bulls are bred to optimize performance in their calves used for consumption. Every once in a while, you will get a breed bull who flat-out fires and becomes a great bucking bull, aka Bodacious. So in our minds, we were doing them a favor because if we found a bull that truly bucked, we could make them some money by finding someone to buy that bull. That wasn't truly our thought process, but just in case one of our old neighbors reads this book, then that's the story we will run with.

One day, my senior year in high school, we decided to buck some of Ben Sharp's young three- and four-year-old Black Angus breed bulls to see if he had any bucking prospects. Don't worry; Ben gave us full permission to buck them. The funny thing with breed bulls, especially Black Angus, is they can be a tad lazy at times. Let me rephrase that. They can be a tad lazy *most* of the time. If it doesn't involve a shade tree, water, food, a group of cows, or whipping another bull off for that group of cows, they don't want anything to do with it. This includes bucking. That still didn't deter us from trying.

By this time in our lives, my brother had already broken his neck and was in a wheelchair. He has this knack, still to this day, of being able to get other people to do highly dangerous, idiotic things for the entertainment of himself and everyone else watching. To get them to do it, he will totally pull the "I would do it if I could, but I'm in a wheelchair" card. The truth is, I know him, and I know he *would* do it if he could. I think that is why friends are so willing to try these insane stunts. Add in the fact that we truly *are* crazy, so deep down it sounds exciting anyway.

To see what my brother has gone through in his life – to not settle for his circumstance but to simply adjust his trajectory and stay the course – has been enough to fuel me to keep fighting through my injuries, which are minor in comparison.

Life will throw us curveballs. This could be as a result of our own decisions, or it could be the result of some random action out of our control. We all have a choice to make in that moment. No matter what the curveball is, or what the circumstances have entailed, you can either let that one moment in your life *define* who you are or let it *fine tune* who you are. People can either know you for the rest of your life as the result of that circumstance or they can recognize that circumstance as a moment in your life that made you stronger. The choice is up to you.

You, ultimately, are who is in control of your own destiny. Other people can put roadblocks in your way. Your childhood could put you farther behind the starting block than others. Circumstances in life could completely reroute your GPS in an instant. But the question you must ask yourself is, "Am I ok with settling with this as my life, or am I willing to put in the work to overcome this moment in my life and still be successful?"

Most people are all too willing to *accept* their life and not *lead* their life. They love to talk about change, but change takes work most people are not willing to put in. Former Professional American Football player JJ Watt put it perfectly when he stated, "Success is not owned, it is leased; and the rent is due every day.[1]" To be successful you must be willing to work daily towards that goal no matter what outside circumstances are thrown your way.

People may still only recognize you for that one moment in life. You have to be willing to accept that reality. Some people can never get their mind past what happened. But you still have the choice to let that moment become the definition of who you are, or a reference in the back of the book about your life. Are you willing to dust yourself off, learn from the mistakes you may have made that got you into that situation, and adjust your course accordingly to move past that moment with growth? These are questions you must constantly ask yourself.

When it comes to facing adversity, you have to evaluate your internal attitude on a regular basis.

---

1. Neumann, Thomas. "Top 10 Quotes: J.J. Watt's Greatest Hits." *ESPN*, ESPN Internet Ventures, 17 Nov. 2015, www.espn.com/nfl/story/_/id/14155141/houston-texans-jj-watt-inspires-list-top-10-quotes-andy-dalton-quip.

"Do I want to quit, or do I want to keep moving forward?"

"Am I going to settle, or am I going to adjust?"

"Am I doing everything I can to change my situation?"

"Is what I say out of my mouth matching up with what I want for my future or just complaining about my situation?"

I have a quote I have learned to live by. "Work like it depends on you. Pray like it depends on God." I don't know who the original author of the quote is, but it has become my motto in life. It is one of those quotes that hits you in the face the moment you hear it because you know the truth behind it, and the potential impact it could have on your situation. You can't have one without the other when it comes to life-changing circumstances. You can't sit and pray for God to bring a miracle while you do nothing. Faith without action is dead.

I truly believe some things in life you can never achieve without God stepping in. That has been the entirety of my life. I would not be where I am today if not for my faith in God. I wouldn't be able to look past the insane obstacles I have faced, and still face on a seemingly constant basis, had I not put my faith in God in all situations, every day, and in every matter I put my mind to. Some days, when the effects of concussions reared their darkest head, which we will get into in later chapters, my faith in God was the *only* thing that got me through it.

Some moments in life can only *seem* life-changing. Others can truly *be* life-changing; none more so than that afternoon bucking those breeding bulls in the arena at our ranch.

Sometimes we had numerous people at our house, riding and helping. Other times I would get an itch to practice, and it would be only my dad around to help. My dad would pull my bull rope then I would sit and wait while he hopped down into the arena to open the chute gate for me. This day was one of those days. My brother parked his wheelchair in his normal spot where he would sit and watch beside the bucking chutes just outside of the arena. On that day, I rode breed bull after breed bull. Not a single one bucked. They either ran across the arena kicking at their belly or they stood flat-footed and spun circles trying to figure out what was going on. With each bull I got on that day, the more relaxed I became, because I was starting to realize there wasn't a single bull in this crop of breed bulls that would actually buck.

After eight or nine bulls, I considered calling it a day, but we still had one breed bull I wanted to try. His breed-registered name was Dakota Cash, but we called him Dakota for short. He was larger than the other bulls. This was a potential downside because if he truly bucked then we would only get a few years out of him before he got too heavy to keep bucking. Besides, he was worth quite a bit as a breed bull in his own right. But the State High School Finals Rodeo was coming up the following weekend and I needed the practice. I figured since the other bulls didn't buck, he wouldn't either. But bull riding is about training muscle memory through repetition. So, what harm could be done by riding one more bull that was probably just going to run off anyways?

You will excuse me if I didn't try to ride Dakota as hard as I typically would try to ride any other bull. I thought he was going to be like all the other breed bulls we bucked that day. Boy, was I wrong. My brother said that was one of the rankest trips he had ever seen any bull have in person up to that point. If you knew my brother, then you would know how much weight that comment carries. Many would consider him one of the world's leading experts on bucking bulls due to the amount of time he has spent with his online bucking bull auction company, The Breeder's Connection. So when he says a bull had an overly rank trip, I believe him.

To back up a moment, I started wearing a helmet before it was "cool." I caught a horn between the eyes when I was 11 years old that sliced me open straight to the bone. Shortly after that, I watched live on television as Brent Thurman had a bull step on the back of his head during the 10th and final round of the NFR. Brent died later that day. After that it was an easy decision to start wearing a helmet. In today's rodeo world, the majority of bull riders wear helmets, but in the late 1990s barely anyone did. In fact I rode with one of the very first prototypes of the Bull Tough Helmet, with the clear visor on the facemask. In the arena at our ranch that summer day, my senior year in high school, the Bull Tough Helmet I was wearing saved my life.

I got on Dakota four times in my career, all in the practice pen since I never drew him at a rodeo we both performed at. One of the best bull rides I ever made was on him in front of only my dad and one other person without anyone videoing it. We were able to capture the second time I covered him on video but, while he still bucked hard, he didn't have his normal amazing trip. Dakota was never ridden at a rodeo during his short career. One of my favorite personal achievements is that I was able to cover him those two times in the practice pen. This first time he bucked was definitely *not* one of those times.

He caught me completely off guard. To be honest with you, even if I had been prepared, I think it would have been the same result with the trip he had that day. My recollection of that day is very blurry, but the parts I do remember, I remember vividly as if it happened yesterday. Just sitting here thinking of it right now, I can still feel the same pain, hear the same sounds, and smell the same smells as if I was experiencing it today.

Dakota bailed out of the chute, kicked over his head, and cranked it back to the right as soon as his front feet hit the ground. With every jump, he got stronger than the jump before, maintaining his tight spin while getting higher in the air and kicking harder each time. Just a few wraps after my dad opened the gate, I was on the end of my arm and being yard-darted headfirst into the ground. Dakota was spinning on top of me still bucking just as hard. As I started to get to my hands and knees to crawl away, I remember seeing two hind feet out of the corner of my eye headed straight for my head.

My very next memory was crawling on my hands and knees, with the helmet no longer on my head, towards my brother who was sitting on the other side of the fence. I was in shock. All I could hear were the sounds of a thousand telephones ringing in my ears. My head hung down and my mouth stayed open, as I was completely numb and "tingly" all over. My whole face felt like when your leg starts to wake from its sleep. I could feel and see the blood trickling from my mouth and ears, down my face, and onto the ground in front of me. I didn't know what had happened, but I knew it was serious.

When a bull is bucking, it is hard to comprehend just how much power is coiled up in their back legs from the momentum of the kick transitioning back to the ground as their legs slingshot in the spin down for the next jump. I cannot even begin to explain the sheer force a bull's back legs use when they make contact with the ground to begin that next jump. In this situation, both of Dakota's back feet were close together. On his transition down, both hind feet hit square on the right side of my helmet, one towards the top of the head and the other lined up perfectly with the ear hole. His feet gathered my head up with them and slammed my head into the ground, sandwiching it between his feet and the dirt.

Bull Tough Helmets are indestructible. They are designed to absorb any blows to the head or face, and almost always do their job without failure. I have never heard of this happening any other time, but the force was so strong that it crushed my helmet, cracking it into two pieces as a result. I wore my glasses under my helmet that day. Not only did it mangle them but it also popped both lenses completely out of my glasses. Twelve years later, my dad was tilling up the arena and saw something flashy in the dirt. He found one of my lenses laying a few dozen yards from where the accident occurred.

This incident also strengthens my belief in the power of prayer. That day my mom, who was in the house, got a call from a lady in our church. As soon as my mom answered the phone, the lady said "Is Nick ok?!" When my mom asked what she was talking about, the woman said, "I had a strong urge to pray for Nick immediately and stopped everything I was doing to pray." At that very moment, while on the phone, my mom looked out of the kitchen window towards the arena at the bottom of the hill and saw me crawling towards my brother without a helmet on my head.

Since that day, I can't hear too well out of my right ear. I quickly learned how to read lips, which makes trying to understand people from Louisiana and deep South Texas even harder since some of them never move their lips when they talk.

I had to miss the State High School Finals Rodeo, and as a result, the National High School Finals Rodeo. It was my senior year, so that was almost as painful as the incident itself. I took around three weeks off then was back at it again. But since I didn't give myself enough time for my resulting severe concussion to heal, this moment became the beginning of what would be a very rough next five years.

Chapter 4

The Snowball Effect

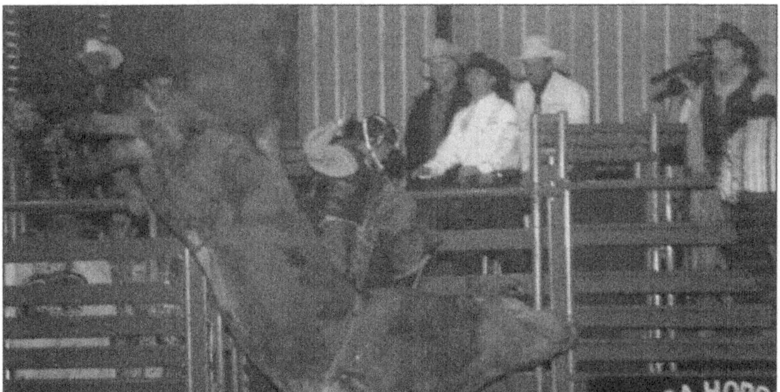

Nick (18) on Bam Bam of Bierema Rodeo Company This photo is taken seconds before Nick cracked the C-2 vertebrae in his neck. Photo courtesy of Plooster Photography

"Cowboy up."

That was the story of my early life, and many rodeo cowboys' lives. "Cowboy up. Stop whimpering about your pains. Get to the next rodeo."

This mentality would be a major contributing factor to why I accrued so many injuries in such a short period of time. In rodeo, an athlete isn't getting paid if they aren't competing. It's not like other professional sports where the athlete keeps getting a paycheck while they are healing-up on an injured reserve list. Or where they get paid regardless of whether they win or lose. In rodeo, athletes must be on the road constantly, one event after another. Most importantly, they must keep placing high enough to win any money. There is no guarantee of getting paid as their pay is 100% contingent on their performance, the performance of the animal they have drawn, and how they place based on their combined performance; considering the rider even got a qualified ride to earn a score. If a bull rider is laid up nursing an injury, then he isn't getting on any bulls and therefore he isn't giving himself a chance to be paid. So, as a bull rider, you find yourself riding through all types of injuries no matter what the consequences may be. For instance, when I broke T10 and T11 in my back, I sat out only eight weeks. We made a hard brace that held my back straight and in place. Then, after only two months, I was back to riding bulls at the most elite level of our sport.

We tend to equate fighting through injuries with being tough, especially in a sport like rodeo. Rodeo athletes take *pride* in competing through their injuries. It becomes a badge of honor and respect of how tough you really are. Rodeo cowboys don't want to be perceived as weak amongst their peers, so we don't give in to our injuries. We just keep taking it one day at a time, blocking out the pain. The downside of this is that while we are trying to protect the already hurt parts of our bodies, we are subconsciously putting more stress on the *rest* of the body and exposing other areas for a potentially new injury.

A prime example of this was when I dislocated my shoulder the night before the accident that resulted in a cracked C-2 vertebrae in my neck. This wasn't that big of a deal to me; shoulder dislocations had been an ongoing issue that whole year. Besides, it was the easier of the two shoulders to relocate whenever it did come out. When it happened that night, I walked briskly back behind the chutes so I wouldn't show pain inside the arena. I grabbed my wrist with my left hand and lifted my arm up to the highest rung of the panel in front of me that I could, which was just a little over waist high. My friend standing there with me held my right hand tight to the panel, then I yanked back and down to my knees, popping the shoulder back into place. Once the pain subsided, I kept my arm close to my body the rest of the night then rotated ice and heat on it back at the hotel.

We were at the SDRA Finals that weekend. The SDRA (South Dakota Rodeo Association) is an amateur association I grew up riding in. Back then it was an *extremely* competitive organization with numerous current and future NFR Qualifying athletes, as well as future PRCA World Champions, competing. In fact a future 2-Time World Champion Saddle Bronc Rider, Chad Ferley, pulled my rope for me on this particular night.

It is amazing to look back at that time in South Dakota rodeo and reminisce on how many NFR Qualifications, PRCA World Championships, Timed Event World Championships, and INFR World Championships would eventually be won by the group of high school athletes in western South Dakota from that era. I personally believe it is one of the better crops of high school talent culminating from one small area that we have ever seen: simply by the sheer *number* of talented rodeo athletes at that time; especially the crop of saddle bronc riders from South Dakota in that era. South Dakota rodeo fans also took notice of the talent they were witnessing. SDRA rodeos carried such a large fan base at the time that the SDRA Finals were broadcast live on prime-time television across the state, and thousands of fans attended the Finals in person. Much of the livestock we were getting on were also being hauled to professional rodeos. So, with the level of talent combined with the level of stock this was a highly entertaining event.

I had turned 18 years old a couple months earlier and had only been to a couple professional rodeos at this point. I had a very blessed spring and led the SDRA standings most of that year despite missing significant time from a few injuries, including the head injury mentioned in the previous chapter. Going into the Finals, it was a tight race between myself and three other friends. I placed in the first round but bucked off in the second round, leaving the door wide open for my friends to pass me if I didn't have a good final round the next day. I had to make a decision by morning if I was going to even get on in the third round or be forced to withdraw based on how my shoulder felt. It still felt loose inside the socket throughout the night. Everything in me knew I needed to turn out of the event.

But I had also drawn a bull I had wanted to get on my whole life: Bam Bam of Harvey Bierema's. Bam Bam was somewhat of a local legend I had grown up watching. In fact, he is still considered a legend by many in South Dakota to this day. I had never drawn him before, and it would turn out to be the only time I would draw him in my entire career. For that reason alone, I made the decision to ride despite the shoulder not feeling fully stable yet.

Bam Bam did his thing, turning back into my hand as soon as the gate opened. For those of you not familiar with rodeo terminology, the term "into my hand" refers to a bull spinning in the direction of whichever hand you are hanging onto the bullrope with. So, for me, since I rode bulls with my left hand, "into my hand" would be a bull spinning to the left and "away from my hand" would be a bull spinning to the right. When a bull is spinning into a rider's hand, the correct move to make with their free hand – the hand not in the bullrope – is to throw it over their head at the crest of the jump and while the bull is in his kicking motion. This motion, unfortunately, is not comfortable for a shoulder that had been dislocated just 16 hours earlier.

I anticipated this going into the ride. So, I tried to make a minor adjustment, moving my arm at an angle that I knew wouldn't put much stress on the shoulder but would also help me make the corners without turning my shoulders or hips out of position. About four or five seconds into the ride, I could feel my shoulder moving around inside the socket, on the brink of dislocating again. I tried tucking my elbow in closer to the side of my body to keep the shoulder from moving. That move dipped my right shoulder, which got me a little behind, and my hips got out of shape to the right. With my free-arm elbow tucked-in to my side, I couldn't make the move I needed to cut that corner and realign my hips – looking over my left shoulder, dipping that left shoulder, throwing my free arm behind my head, and releasing my outside leg while simultaneously shifting my hips to the left. Instead I shifted more to the right and got thrown the next jump, flipping backwards. Usually when a rider is bucked off, he tries to use his arms as a sort of spring to absorb the impact of the ground on the fall and to continue the momentum to rotate and land as close to his hands and knees as possible. Because I was doctoring my shoulder, I pulled my arm closer to my side and hand to my chest. Instead of absorbing the blow with both of my hands and completing the rotation, I now took the full impact of the ground on the top back corner of my head.

On impact, it felt like someone had just electrocuted me. A shock coursed through my entire body and out every extremity. I laid there for a split second, then rolled to my knees. Everything felt numb but I still had feeling. I told myself I had merely rung my bell, not giving a single thought to the fact that it could be a serious injury. In rodeo – and most of the sports world – "getting your bell rung" is a term that has long been used to refer to the temporary confusion, disorientation, and ringing in the ears that follows a blow to the head. It also becomes an all-too-easy scapegoat to brush off what could be a potentially serious injury.

I refused to acknowledge my injury that day. I didn't even let an EMT look at me. I was too mad at myself for letting the year-end title go, even though one of my traveling partners beat me out for it by less than $50. But the rest of that day, any time I turned my head, that same electric shock coursed through my body. I chalked it up as a pinched nerve: a common nagging injury in the rodeo world.

I let my friends pack my equipment for me before we headed home. That six-hour drive in the passenger seat was miserable. Every bump we hit felt like someone was sitting behind me with a Taser pulling the trigger.

The next day, I felt even worse. My college rodeo coach called me into his office and told me he wouldn't let me ride at the next college rodeo the following weekend until I went and got my neck examined. No matter how hard I tried to convince him it was only a "stinger", he insisted I wasn't competing until I got it checked. I had only been in college for a few weeks at this point. With only 10 rodeos in a College Rodeo Season, missing just one would hurt me in the standings. After placing well at the first college rodeo a week earlier, I wanted to build on that momentum. I didn't want to risk him benching me, so I begrudgingly complied and went to get my neck examined. Boy, am I glad he convinced me to go to the doctor!

The X-rays showed a partial crack across C-2 and the beginnings of what is called a Hangman's Fracture. The spinal cord hadn't been touched so at least there weren't any injuries to it. But what the doctor told me next shook me to my core. Many people don't live through a C-1 or C-2 fracture. It is called a Hangman's Fracture because it replicates the fracture incurred during a judicial hanging. If a person does survive this injury, it is typically with full-body paralysis. Thankfully, mine was only a partial crack that never developed into a full fracture, nor did any damage to the spine. I thank God that was the only extent of this injury, as it could have been much, much worse.

To this day, I have a small bone spur where the injury occurred on C-2 as a reminder of my stupidity to not get it checked immediately. Every time I have gone to a new chiropractor, and they do the initial X-ray, they always freak out a little bit when they see that bone spur. Almost all of them refuse to even touch my neck for an adjustment after taking an X-ray.

We have deduced that my current issues with passing out frequently may not be fully due to concussions, but possibly a combination of the concussions and the tension in my neck from this injury. Either one can cause light-headedness and inner-ear equilibrium issues. Both combined together are a mixed drink of misery.

People ask me all the time if I regret riding bulls or if I had a "do-over", would I take a different path. The answer is I would absolutely ride bulls again and I don't regret taking that path one iota. If I had a do-over, I *would* do a few things differently though. For instance, I would take more time off to let my injuries heal. That's my only regret: that I was too narrow-mindedly focused on my short-term goals to see the longevity of getting healthy and staying healthy. I had my fair share of injuries. It was a roller coaster of emotions and frustrations. I knew if I could just stay healthy, I would have a very bright future. But you can't *stay* healthy if you don't *let yourself heal first.*

At the time, I thought it was the "tough" thing to do: to ride through an injury. Now I believe the exact opposite. I think the "tough" thing to do is to let yourself heal, even if it means ridicule from your peers. I believe now that it takes a tougher man to say, "I need to let my injury heal", when everyone else is telling you to "cowboy up", than it does to cave to other people's opinions. You must remember this is *your* body, not theirs. I was so concerned about other people's opinions and worried about looking weak in their eyes if I didn't ride while hurt. You know what? I don't see a *single one* of these people in my life now. They moved on. I moved on. In the totality of it, their opinion never mattered. But I didn't see that then. I was blinded by something we all chase: acceptance. I took pride in the fact that they all thought I was tough.

Now I'm not talking about the little nagging injuries. You are going to have nagging injuries that never go away anytime you are competing at a high level in *any* sport. I'm not saying every little pain or soreness means you need to rest. But the serious injuries definitely need to be taken seriously. Concussions are a far more serious injury than they seem at the time. The brain, the heart, and the spine are the three areas a person doesn't want to leave unchecked, especially if potential long-term damage is suspected. You must *make* yourself take time to heal because, as any competitor will tell you, nothing in your inner drive wants to stop.

Here is something I have found out about concussions. When you receive one, it is almost like a trigger goes off in your brain that makes you rationalize in your mind that there is no reason for you to stop competing. If anything, it makes you want to compete even more. It's like you have a task that went unfinished, and your motor won't stop running until you can finish that task. You need someone else to take action to make you stop. Football players who receive concussions now have their helmets hidden from them to prevent them from running back onto the field despite being told not to. Athletes don't want to quit. They want to compete. For some reason, a concussion amplifies that need to finish what we started.

This trigger-response doesn't only happen when competing either. Just recently I was at my house walking something to the trash can. I got lightheaded, passed out, and hit my head on the way to the ground. When I came to, it was my mission in life to get to that trash can and throw away whatever it was I needed to throw away. Something triggered in my mind telling me the most important thing in the world was finishing the task I was doing when I hit my head. My wife had to practically sit on top of me to stop me from trying to get to that trash can. She literally had to take the trash from my hand, then make sure I *saw* her throwing it away, before my brain would let me feel comfortable enough to lay there and recover. Now, throwing my banana peel into the trash won't – or shouldn't – reinjure my brain, but this 'must finish' trigger pushes athletes to compete when they should be stopping to recover. The drive is so strong and unrelenting that athletes cannot be trusted to self-assess their own injuries. They are powerless to ignore the concussed brain's 'get it done at all costs' trigger.

Before we knew a lot about concussions, there wasn't anybody truly making athletes stop and rest if they sustained a hard blow to the head. In fact, in the rodeo world, we were encouraged to "cowboy up" and keep going. So that's what I did. I kept riding. I ignored the symptoms, ignored the side effects, and kept doing the same thing over and over again. I cannot emphasize this next point enough! If you have a loved one who gets a concussion, step in and be the mediator who convinces them to rest. They need *you* to be that person because they can't be that person themselves.

Here is the tricky thing about concussions. If you don't let them completely heal, it is a whole lot easier to get another one. When I speak at school assemblies or to young athletes, I always tell them, "However long your doctor tells you to take off from a concussion; double it. If they tell you 4 weeks, take 8. If they tell you 3 months, take 6." Why do I recommend taking double the time? Because when it comes to letting the brain fully heal, you cannot be too cautious.

Repeated concussions are a scary thing. Once you start getting a few consecutive concussions, it becomes progressively easier to keep getting more. Just like a snowball rolling downhill; the longer you keep adding on concussions in succession, the faster you get them and the bigger they are. If you don't take that extra time to let your brain heal, you open yourself up to more concussions on a more consistent basis.

Your brain has a chance to recover if you *force* yourself to take time off to let it recover *fully*. But if you don't let it recover, you will get to a point of no return … the place where the true concussion issues begin. What do you have to lose by taking extra time off? That was a hard thing for me to grasp. I totally get it now that I am older and can look back at my life. But in the moment, I was more concerned about what I was missing when healing up rather than buying into the vision that by taking that extra time off to heal now, I could extend my career in the future. I would gladly go back and miss a few extra months if it meant my career could have lasted past 21 years old.

But I didn't see that future. I was too focused on the "now." I would get knocked out and go on to the next rodeo like nothing happened. Every knockout seemed to have a different reaction or result. During some knockouts, my entire body would go completely stiff. During other knockouts, my body would go completely limp.

Some were so severe I even went into a full "fencing response."

In the medical community, the fencing response is called asymmetrical tonic neck reflex, or ATNR. The reason why this involuntary reflex became known as the fencing response is because it's the same position a fencer takes when taking the 'en garde' stance in a fencing bout; with both arms in front of them, one fully extended and the other bent at the elbow. The human body unconsciously assumes the ATNR position when the higher cerebral cortex has experienced a shock or injury. This is the part of the brain that's responsible for vital involuntary functions such as breathing, body temperature regulation, and heart rate.[1]

Most commonly, an ATNR response occurs when the soft brain tissue slams into the skull during an acceleration or deceleration injury. When the higher cerebral cortex becomes bruised, it momentarily shuts itself down. Thankfully, the brain has a backup plan. The primitive brain stem jumps in and takes control of those basic, but necessary, body functions, like breathing. It typically doesn't take long before the cerebral cortex recovers from its initial shock and resumes working, despite the bruising of the soft issue. The fencing position, however, is an

1. Gotter, Ana. "Fencing Response: What It Is, Why It Occurs, and Why It Matters." *Healthline,* Healthline Media, 13 May 2025, www.healthline.com/health/fencing-response.

outward indication that the injury was severe enough for this temporary transfer of brain function to occur.[2] With what I know about brain injuries now, it is extremely scary for me to look back at how many times I have been knocked-out so hard that I went into the fencing position; more times than I can count.

One time, I got jerked down onto a bull's head so hard it bent my helmet's metal facemask and knocked me out cold. But I stayed on his back, sat up, and my body kept naturally making the necessary moves while he spun into my hand. I kept riding him even after the whistle blew. It wasn't until I hit the ground and didn't move, that people even realized I was knocked out. I somehow finished 1st at that rodeo and pulled a good check. That fact alone makes it one of my favorite memories to this day — or would it be called a non-memory since I was technically knocked out the whole time?

Eventually, it got to where the simplest things would knock me out: like landing on the ground too hard or hitting the back of my head on the trunk door from standing up too soon after putting my gear bag away. But I kept plugging away, not letting myself heal, and letting those concussions stack on top of each other.

Not every concussion during this period was rodeo-related though. Some of them go back to that need for

---

2. Gotter

adrenaline. One of our traditions for our College Rodeo Team was "waterslide sledding". When the first hard freeze made its way into South Dakota, we hopped the fence to the local outdoor waterslide park in Rapid City. We spent a couple nights clearing the snow out of the slides then pouring water up and down them to form a hard, icy surface. Then at the bottom we stacked snow like a ramp and poured water over it to freeze as a jump. After that, we spent quite a few nights in a row sledding in the dark well into the morning. The slides we would always sled on were lined up side-by-side and went straight down the hill, without any turns, but had three "rounded steps" on the way down so it looked like a large, curvy staircase going down the hill. Typically in the summertime, visitors would line up next to a friend on each of the slides and race down in the water. But during our "waterslide sledding" days in the wintertime, we raced down them on plastic, disc-shaped sleds and an iced up surface. If we got enough speed, we could actually "skip" down the slide barely touching each step on the way down. Side by side could get a tad dangerous if one person lost balance, because they flew off the side and typically collided with the person on the other slide. As you can probably see, this was an absolute blast! Year after year, we built on this tradition with our jumps at the bottom getting bigger.

One night there were just a few of us there at the slides getting them prepared for the traditional races. When we finished making the best jump we could possibly make at the bottom, and icing the slides up to the extreme, we decided to give them a few test runs. These were undoubtedly the fastest slides we had made to date. The second to last pass down, I almost skipped the final step altogether. So, of course, I had to accept that challenge and see if I could get even more speed to actually clear it this time. I got a massive running start and dove headfirst into my plastic disc. I was able to keep full contact on the first step, which was crucial to building the most speed. Because of that momentum, I got a massive jump off the second step. Still in the air, I barely clipped the third step with the back of the disc on my way over. This made my disc nose-dive down and caused me to slide down the last part of the slide with full contact of my disc, which in turn caused me to build up even more speed than usual.

In the summer, the bottom portion of the slide is designed to slow riders down. In the winter, we bypassed this with ice to gain even more speed going into our big jump … the last jump before landing into the snow-filled pool at the end.

On my epic run, I picked up way too much speed and tried to adjust my weight to slow down. At about that same time, I launched off the man-made jump. Because I shifted my weight, the sled started to turn upside down on me in the air. I remember pitching the sled, flying through the air, desperately flailing my arms and legs while hoping to find a soft spot to land. I realized I was going to miss the pool altogether and I came crashing down on the cement walkway on the other side of the pool.

My very next memory was sitting in class the next day with zero recollection of how I got there. Dustin Luper, one of my best friends who was also there with me, swears I cleared at least 50 feet before having the most glorious crash he had ever seen. By the time they got to me, they said I was knocked out cold. According to my friends on the scene, after I came to, we had a few laughs over the crash, hopped the fence, and went back to Dustin's house for some hot chocolate; none of which I remember. While most concussions were a result of rodeo, as you can see, I was also my own worst enemy, thanks to adrenaline, fearlessness, and my willingness to do "crazy things".

With each concussion, my side effects worsened. I found myself constantly tired, always having a headache, and consistently nauseous no matter how many times I threw up. Somewhere in the mix of these concussions, I developed vertigo. If you think vertigo is weird enough as it is, try having it kick-in while you are on the back of a spinning bull. I couldn't believe what I was seeing in the weird tricks my eyes were playing on me at that moment.

Looking back, concussions were all part of the sport and the mentality of the lifestyle that accompanies it. You are going to get hurt. You are going to get knocked out. Cowboy up and move on.

I have since come to despise the term "cowboy up."

Chapter 5

My Introduction to Temporary Amnesia

Nick (19) on Black Cat of Waln Rodeo Company one year to the day after cracking the C-2 vertebrae in his neck.
Photo Courtesy of Cathy Morrison

It's a scary feeling when I can't piece things together.

There is this distant feeling that you "know you should know", but no matter how hard I try, my brain hits a wall at a certain point every time. Sometimes that wall moves a little further away, revealing more as time passes. Other times, it seems like that wall is immovable and I will never be able to remember.

I didn't always have problems with this. In fact, outside of the isolated incident in this chapter, it took years before temporary amnesia became a regular issue at all. Until the last dozen or so years, it would be tied exclusively to a moment when I would get knocked out. Now it just simply happens. Sometimes it is triggered by moments of stress, while other times it is triggered by too many things going on all at once. If I am in a room with a lot of kids running around, everyone doing a commotion of different things, or multiple conversations taking place simultaneously, it is like my brain can't process everything so it decides to "shut down" instead.

Sometimes all I do is look down then look up, and my brain will think I am in a different location than I really am. The easiest way to describe this feeling is a "dream jump." Have you ever been deep into a dream and see something similar to another thought, which causes your entire dream to shift gears to a whole new plot and location? It's like that, but it happens in real life. I will see something familiar and my brain will "dream jump" to another location. But now my eyes are not matching what my brain is thinking, which sends me into a tailspin of confusion. For simplicity's sake, whenever this happens my wife and I have started calling them "brain episodes."

I have to consciously prevent my mind from panicking so the confusion doesn't accelerate. If I panic, that confusion leads to not trusting my own thoughts, which in turn leads to forgetting even more things around me. I have to make an intentional effort to not spiral down this hole. It becomes a battle between my mind not wanting to trust what I am seeing or hearing, and forcing myself to trust those things.

For instance, one time we were in a fast food drive-thru in one town. After picking up our order, I started to pull out of the parking lot, but my brain "jumped" to the same fast food restaurant but in a *different* town. So, while I assumed I should see familiar roads and buildings, my eyes were looking at a completely different view than what I *thought* I should be seeing. I couldn't comprehend at the moment that I was in a different town, so I immediately panicked. I didn't know where I was, even though I did a mere two minutes ago. Even after I asked my family where we were, it was still difficult for me to wrap my head around why we would be hundreds of miles away from where I thought we were. My mind was convinced we are not only in a different town, but that we had been there all day.

I believe this "dream jump" happens because I have a hard time differentiating between my dream world and the real world. This has equal parts to do with my dreams being so realistic and my reality being so dream-like. Most people who have had multiple concussions report having a "cloudy" or "foggy" feeling. For some, it is temporary, while for others, it is constant. Mine goes back as far as I can remember.

It seems the less sleep I get, the foggier I feel. While that feeling never fully goes away, I try to combat it by getting an adequate amount of sleep every night. This is easier said than done. Many nights, I am startled awake, covered in sweat, because I am convinced my dream is happening in reality. Add in the fact that, to be functional on a day-to-day basis, I must do two to four hours of brain exercises and rehab first thing every morning, and sleep now becomes more of a luxury than a commodity.

No matter what triggers these brain episodes, it is never a fun experience to live through. If my nose starts to bleed, it is usually a forewarning that one is going to happen either immediately or in the next hour or two. Nosebleeds aren't fun, but I prefer them over having no warning of an impending brain episode. At least the nosebleed gives me and my wife a heads up so we can prepare accordingly. If I am driving, I will pull over and let her drive. If we are walking around somewhere, then we will find an air-conditioned location to sit and rest, hopefully minimizing the severity of the brain episode. If

I am home, we will turn off all the lights and black out the windows, as an ear-splitting migraine and vomiting are sure to follow.

Sometimes I recognize the people around me, but don't recognize the area I am in. Sometimes I recognize the area, but don't recognize the people. Other times, I don't recognize either. In the worst scenarios – thankfully, rare events – I won't even recognize myself. One person I have never forgotten, to this date, is my wife. If I see her or hear her voice, she becomes a rock I latch onto in that moment. She recognizes the confusion in my eyes and tells me the small details that help me piece together the puzzle I am trying to solve in my mind. While none of it makes sense at the moment, it still helps me understand my surroundings and lessens the confusion until my mind starts to come back around.

From experience and observation, my wife has figured out that my mind typically jumps back three years when this happens. So, if we have moved within the past three years, I won't recognize our own house when we pull into the driveway after a brain episode, or I will think we are visiting a friend's house if it happens when we are already home. I have to fight back tears whenever I don't recognize my own children, and then feel like I have missed watching them grow up because my last memory of them was when they were far younger. Experiencing this breaks my heart for people with Alzheimer's disease. I eventually get my memory back, whereas they are typically stuck in that loop of confusion.

My closest friends try to take advantage of this if they recognize it happening. That's what best friends do. Let me explain the difference between good friends and best friends in the cowboy world. Good friends will see their buddy get into a wreck on the ranch and immediately rush to help them. Best friends – those who will be carrying their casket at their funeral – see their buddy get in a wreck, and delay helping because they are too busy wiping the tears of laughter from their eyes. If they are out doctoring calves and their buddy gets mucked out by a wild mama cow, who doesn't realize we are helping her baby, good friends will try to get that cow to stop hooking their buddy. Best friends? One already has the phone out filming the incident and hollering, "*Don't weaken!*" while another is trying to get that mama to run back over their friend who is balled up on the ground. All three friends are finding it hard to breathe from laughing the entire time. That's just how best friends are.

So how do my best friends take advantage of a brain episode? One night at a busy restaurant, my buddy, Destin, recognized the confusion in my eyes and realized I was experiencing a brain episode. I didn't recognize him, but I was trying to play it off because I didn't know that he knew I was struggling to piece together everything around me. Does he fill me in on his knowledge of my predicament? No. Does he tell my wife, "Hey, I think

Nick is braining out on us"? Nope. Instead, he leans over to me and says, "I'm so excited you agreed to go get a tattoo with me at the parlour around the corner after dinner. I can't believe you picked a butterfly on your lower back, but hey, to each his own. It's gonna be *epic*!" I may not know much at the moment, but I know that ain't happening! So we both burst out laughing because now I know, "I may not recognize this guy, but he must be one of my best friends."

Now that I have had brain episodes happen numerous times, I have learned to cope in the moment. Even though I may be in a full state of confusion, I still understand what is happening. I know that if I can take my time to process the information around me, eventually I will gather all of my chickens back into the coop and get a better understanding of the things I can't yet completely grasp.

All brain injuries are different, so I can only speak on my own personal plethora of experience. Hopefully what I have learned can help you find nuggets that can aid you if you struggle with this as well. When I am trying to get my memory back, I have learned not to panic over the things I don't know. I have to focus on the things I *can* figure out first and use those as the building blocks to recovery. If I let a small amount of panic set in, then it becomes easy for panic to completely take over. Once that happens, my mind goes from building on the things around me I *can* remember to fixating on the things I don't recognize at all. Controlling *where* my focus lies is crucial in recovering. It is important to keep calm and focused while in the moment. If I handle this correctly, then people around me may not even notice anything is amiss, and life will go on as usual once I get my mind back to normal.

If you deal with these same issues, the best advice I can recommend to you is to have a full understanding of your surroundings before it happens. Know where you are, think through the worst-case scenarios, and plan ahead of time before a brain episode happens. Much like knowing every exit of a room in case of an emergency, I assess every room upon entry for my specific circumstances. If I pass out, where are walls, couches, or soft chairs I can lean towards to hopefully break my fall? Are there any glass tables I could fall into that could cause more harm? Where are all the sharp corners I need to avoid? Which areas should I avoid because they echo the most or have the most "chatter" noise? I am attempting to prepare myself to minimize as many side effects as I can in case anything happens.

The best way I have found to prepare myself for a possible brain episode is to write things down. I write them in a place I am certain to look: my phone. Whenever I am confused, I typically grab my phone first to try and find clues about myself. I've noticed I always open the "Notes" icon. My only guess is that I think it will possibly tell me enough about myself to get an idea of who I am. Knowing this, I keep a note pinned at the top that says, "Ask your phone to call your wife. She can help you figure out what is going on". This way if something does happen and I see this note, I can simply ask my phone to "call my wife", even if I don't remember her name, and Ivy is usually on the other end of the line within seconds.

We have started using a locator app on our phones called Life360. It will pinpoint exactly where I am to Ivy, so she can either help guide me home or know where to pick me up. It will also give her notifications when I leave places like home, church, etc. Before we found this app, I had to try to explain to her where I was, which proved to be extremely difficult. This app has been a lifesaver for us!

Now that I have had this happen enough, I have learned to adapt. I can piece things together quicker, and I can stay calm without panicking more often. While today I can still tell, in the back of my head, what is going on, that wasn't the case the first time this happened. I didn't know what to do or what to think. I was merely afraid to say anything to anyone around me because I figured they would think I was making it up. But the very first time I didn't recognize myself I was in the emergency room; not for a head injury but a shoulder injury. This is probably why it was even more confusing to me.

It was my junior year in college. I was at a rodeo less than an hour away from Rapid City where I was going to college. Frankly, I entered it just for fun. I drew a bull with a lot of "drop in the front end." This means he would get a lot of air then his front end would "disappear" as he kicked high over his head with his back legs. These kinds of bulls can be a challenge; always trying to jerk the rope out of your hand, or get you out of position to use their momentum to yank you down onto their head. This can also make them a whole lot of fun to ride.

This bull was spinning to the right, away from my riding hand. With every jump, he would get high in the air and his front end would drop suddenly. He wasn't spinning a tight circle every jump as much as he was jumping forward as he spun, causing him to fade across the arena. These types of bulls really fit my style of riding, so I was having an absolute blast on this bull.

Usually, I had an internal compass telling me where I was in the arena right before getting off my bull after the 8-second buzzer sounded. If anything, I could always pop my head up for a split second to assess my surroundings. Since this bull had so much drop in the front end, I didn't want to lift my head to glance around after the buzzer sounded. It could cause me to lose my center of balance, which could jerk me down onto the bull's head. I was trying to be smart because I didn't want to get knocked out again.

So, I gave my best guess as to where we were. At the peak of his jump, I started the process of "look-throw-kick-let go" (*look* over my left shoulder, *throw* my right arm over my head, *kick* my right knee over his back, and *let go* of the bull rope – all in one motion) to get off into my hand on the left side. If timed correctly, this motion will use the bull's momentum to throw me away from him as I get off.

What I didn't realize was this bull faded more, as he spun during the eight-second ride, than it felt like on his back. He was now farther into the middle of the arena than I had judged with my internal GPS.

The barrelman at this particular rodeo was newer at his job. He didn't do a good enough job of moving his barrel to a better position as my bull faded in his direction. While a barrelman's primary job at a rodeo is to entertain the crowd, his responsibility inside the arena, during the bull riding, is to place his barrel in the best position possible for a bull fighter to use as a basketball-style pick between him and the bull if necessary. This also means keeping it out of the bull's bucking path. The best barrelmen in the business use precision and anticipation to never be in the way, while also being exactly where they are needed to be if a bull fighter gets in a pinch while saving the bull rider. It is, truthfully, an underappreciated skill. It takes years of being in the arena, reading bulls' body language and tendencies, to perfect this skill and intuitively know the precise spot to place the barrel.

Because this particular barrelman had not anticipated my bull's fading path early enough, my bull, while still bucking and spinning, was now on a collision course with his barrel. As I made my get-off move, I immediately saw the barrel blocking my path to the ground. In a split-second decision, I tried catching my right foot against the bull's side to delay my get-off by a jump and miss the barrel. It was too late. My spur caught my rope and the front-end-drop of the bull now slung-shot me harder, yard-darting me right onto the top of the barrel.

My left arm went inside the barrel while the rest of my body slammed against the top and side. The impact dislocated my left shoulder, broke two ribs on my left side under the armpit, and somehow popped my helmet off of my head. It was a mix of pain and excitement as I knew, without a shadow of a doubt, I was going to score enough to win the rodeo with that ride. Yet my dislocated arm was cutting that excitement short as it was quickly reminding me, with throbbing pain, that it was no longer in its socket.

We tried getting the shoulder back into place on our own behind the chutes, but with the broken ribs, it was proving too painful. I begrudgingly agreed to go to the hospital to get the shoulder relocated. My brother happened to be attending this rodeo and wanted to go to the hospital with me. So I waited as our good friend, Jason Hunsaker, helped my brother into the truck, loaded my brother's wheelchair into the back, and then helped me get in. Off to the hospital we went.

One thing to know about dislocations is that the longer your joint is dislocated, the more painful it gets. At some point, the pain becomes unbearable. The longest I have gone with a shoulder dislocated before receiving any pain medication was five and a half hours. It was after the right shoulder came out during a PBR Event in Springfield, Missouri, and I got stuck behind a long waiting list in the emergency room there. It was so painful, towards the end, that I was blacking out from the pain. It gave landing on my spur and splitting my tail-bone a run for its money as the most painful injury during my career. Five and a half hours dislocated without pain meds is a personal record I hope to never come close to breaking again. The dislocation from this story was only out of socket for about two hours. That isn't too bad, but it is still painful enough to make even the toughest of cowboys grit their teeth a little bit.

Usually whenever a patient is in the emergency room after any type of crash, they check for a concussion before administering any medications. This particular time, somebody must not have gotten that memo. Without checking for a concussion, they immediately gave me "soft" pain medication to take the edge off. I wasn't complaining, as it was definitely helpful. But with pain medications also comes the "loopiness". And with the loopiness came an embarrassing moment that involved the pulse oximeter on my finger.

If you don't know what a pulse oximeter is, it's the plastic chip-bag clip they put on the end of your finger at the hospital to measure the oxygen saturation in your blood-stream, as well as your heart rate. Usually, I don't mind the pulse oximeter on my finger. But this particular day, laying in the emergency room bed with a dislocated shoulder and two broken ribs on a light dosage of pain medication, I hated that little truth-telling machine. I hated it because, no matter how hard I tried, it kept giving me away.

Let me explain. I had a very hot nurse tending to me. There is a stereotype out there about how nurses and cowboys always end up dating each other. When you think about how often cowboys ended up in hospitals around nurses, it's easy to see the truth behind this stereotype. My brother and Jason were in the room with me and every time the nurse left the room, all we could talk about was how hot she was. Don't worry, this was well before Jason or I had met our future wives.

The nurse walked into the room to check on me and placed her hand on my leg while she was talking. That stupid machine, with its audible beep....... beep........ beep, started speeding up when she touched my leg. Beep....... beep..... beep... beep... beep... BEEP BEEP!

All I could do was think, *"Slow heart rate. Slow heart rate. Slow heart rate"*. Much to my chagrin, my heart rate would not cooperate. It was embarrassingly obvious. She put her hand on my leg, and the heart monitor sped up. She took her hand off, and it slowed down. Of course, Jason and my brother, being the good friends they are, made this situation worse with their constant pointing out of the heart rate monitor's speed in her presence. Eventually, she caught on and noticed it as well. On a side note, I left the hospital with her phone number, and we dated for a couple months. So, maybe that pulse oximeter wasn't all that bad.

Since somebody had already given me small doses of pain meds, the doctor never checked for a concussion either and approved a full dosage of muscle relaxers so they could relocate my shoulder. I had no idea how something as harmless as that medicine would change things, but it did … from the moment that hot sensation went through my veins surrounding the IV in my arm.

I have learned since this incident that there is a very good reason why doctors are cautious about giving pain medication to a concussed patient. According to a research study that appeared in the September/October 2024 issue of *Military Medicine,* it is generally safe to take acetaminophen – the active ingredient in Tylenol – after a concussion. However, other over-the-counter pain meds, like naproxen in Aleve and ibuprofen in Advil, can increase the chance of bleeding. Even small brain bleeds can cause temporary confusion, memory loss, and impaired cognitive function.[1]

Since I arrived at the ER with a dislocated shoulder and cracked ribs, the medication I was given was a muscle relaxant. I have read medical studies conducted by the Cleveland Clinic, and published on their website, showing that certain types of muscle relaxants, like those with anticholinergic properties, can make the memory and confusion issues that are common with concussions even worse. The anticholinergic properties mess with a neurotransmitter, called acetylcholine, which has a key role in the brain's cognitive and memory function.[2]

We didn't know it at the time, but when I hit that barrel, I incurred a slight concussion. So when I was administered muscle relaxers to aid in relocating the shoulder, it made for a dangerous combination since I wasn't checked for a concussion first.

Typically, when a shoulder is relocated, it is a remarkable feeling. Previously you felt this void in your arm where the shoulder should be that is hard to explain. Muscle

---

1. Lauren Earyes, Yll Agimi, Katharine Stout, Benzodiazepine Prescription Patterns After Mild Traumatic Brain Injury in U.S. Military Service Members, *Military Medicine*, Volume 189, Issue 9-10, September/October 2024, Pages 1931–1937, https://doi.org/10.1093/milmed/usad443
2. "Anticholinergic Drugs: What They Are & How They Work." *Cleveland Clinic*, 30 June 2025, my.clevelandclinic.org/health/treatments/anticholinergic-drugs.

spasms increase this feeling as they try to pull the shoulder into place on their own. When a shoulder is finally relocated, there is this moment of relief that lasts for a few minutes before the true pain from all of the pulling and jarring eventually sets in.

This time, when I woke up, I didn't care about any pain in my arm, but rather that I didn't recognize a single person in the room. I didn't recognize Jason. I didn't recognize my brother. Worst of all, I didn't recognize myself. I remember sitting in that hospital bed trying to figure things out, but I was afraid to say anything. Why I was afraid, I don't think I will ever be able to tell you. I just know for the next few hours, I did a lot of "faking." I faked conversations or the answers to the questions doctors asked me. I gave them what I felt would be an answer they would accept, which apparently they did. I think they simply wrote off any weird actions or looks on my face as still being groggy from the medication.

I don't remember very much of the rest of that day, or even the next two weeks. But I will never forget the feeling of fear I had that moment I woke up.

I pieced together that I should know the cowboy standing in the corner and the guy sitting in the wheelchair beside him. If I could convince them that I had everything in order, then I knew I could pull off this facade that everything was okay. So that became my goal: don't let those two figure out that I don't know who they are.

I heard the name "Nick" being referenced to me so I guessed that was my name. This was the first piece I hung onto to start reconstructing the puzzle in my mind. Within a half hour, I had a full memory of who I was. I now recognized my brother, but I still didn't recognize Jason. By the time I was released from the hospital, I had most things figured out, but not everything. It was all still a big blur.

I vividly remember everything leading up to when I fell asleep for the procedure. Everything after that, and over the next two weeks, is like a haze of "glitched" memories. I slept a lot. Pretty soon, I had things figured out with only occasional moments of forgetfulness. The entire time I had a feeling of an unbalanced equilibrium and brain fog. The closest thing I can compare it to is the cloudiness of extreme jet lag mixed with high dosages of hydrocodone. Dating the nurse I met at the hospital came in extremely handy during this time as she began checking in on me daily. When people would ask why I wasn't in class, I would play it off as "these pain killers are kicking my tail." The reality was that I was experiencing something I had never experienced before. And it scared me.

Thankfully, this was an isolated incident that only lasted a couple of weeks and didn't seem to have any long-term effects. While I now experience memory loss and brain episodes periodically, the temporary amnesia in this instance was way different – and scarier – than what I experience currently.

Once everything subsided, I felt mostly back to normal. It wasn't until what happened in the next chapter that I started to see a noticeable decline in my cognitive or physical skills, and when I started to see the first indicators of the chronic issues I now deal with today.

Chapter 6

When I Got Knocked Out Three Times in One Night

Nick (19) in the short round at the Maverick Stampede College Rodeo in Rapid City, SD on Wild Bill of Eckroth Rodeo Company. Photo Courtesy of JJJ Photography

I have sat here for days trying to remember how much time elapsed between the incident I discussed in the previous chapter and this next one. I would be lying if I said I knew. The reality is the memories of the final three or four years of my bull riding career run so close together in my mind that I almost feel like I have no sense of time during that period of my life. All I know is that this was the incident when everything went from bad to worse. All of my other concussions leading up to this gave me temporary problems. This night was when I started to see long-term, recurring effects.

For those of you unfamiliar with rodeo, I am going to give you a quick Rodeo 101 tutorial. If it is called a "rodeo," then it typically features all of the main disciplines in the sport — bareback riding, steer wrestling, team roping, saddle bronc riding, calf roping, barrel racing, and bull riding. There are many variations to the types of rodeos or events, but that is the main format for most rodeos. If it is simply called a "bull riding", a "barrel racing", a "team roping", etc., then the event will feature only that specific discipline with a higher volume of contestants. So where a rodeo may feature fifteen athletes in each discipline – fifteen bull riders, fifteen barrel racers, fifteen bronc riders, etc. – during a performance, a bull riding will only feature bull riders, with thirty to forty-five competing that night.

Bull riding events themselves can have many different formats. A one-head bull riding means everyone rides one bull and the placings are determined by the scores on that one bull. A two-head, or two-round, bull riding can be in two formats. A less common format is where everyone gets on two bulls and they add the scores together to determine the winner. The most popular format used is a Long Go / Short Go format. Everyone gets on one bull in what is called a long go-round. The short go size is determined before the event starts; usually ten or fifteen. If it is ten, then the riders with the top-ten scores from the long go come back to what is called a short go-round. In the short go they get on the ranker bulls in the pen. The winner of a two-head bull riding is usually determined by their aggregate – their scores added together. Some bull ridings will feature a "winner take all" short round where all the previous scores are thrown out, and the winner is determined solely by their score in the short go.

Another format used in the bigger bull ridings is a three-head, or three-round, format. In this format there are two long go-rounds. Then the riders with the top fifteen aggregate scores, from those two rounds, go on to the short round. Typically, during the long rounds, the bull riders are split into sections of ten bull riders in each section. This gives the riders a better idea of when they will be riding, while also helping the stock contractors know when certain bulls need to be loaded into the chutes.

The night this particular encounter happened was just another bull riding event. It was a three-head format, featuring thirty bull riders in the two long rounds, ten in the short round, and all three rounds taking place in one night. I was scheduled for the first section of the first round and the last section of the second round. I had two really good bulls drawn, so I felt confident about my chances of making it back to the short round and winning a good check.

The first round started out as planned. My bull turned back away from my hand as soon as the gate opened, and faded across the front of the chutes while he spun. Everything felt great. I heard the buzzer, letting me know I made a qualified ride. Then things went south.

Honestly, to this day, I don't know exactly what happened after my ride was over. I got off, and the next thing I remembered was being dazed and rolling onto my hands and knees. I must have landed at a weird angle and temporarily knocked myself out. Witnesses said I hit the ground, laid there completely still for a couple of seconds, and then rolled to my knees and crawled to the fence like nothing happened. I wouldn't have even given it a second thought, but once back in the locker room, I started to feel the same symptoms I felt after a concussion. Upon examination by the doctor on site, it was confirmed I had suffered a concussion.

Thankfully I was one of the first people to ride that day. That meant I had plenty of time to rest before riding again in the 2nd Round, as the competing order is typically swapped between the two rounds. But recovering wasn't coming easy. I had a pounding headache, I was throwing up occasionally, and my vision was extremely blurry. It really wasn't any different than some of the other times I had a concussion. So, I played it off as nothing serious. I decided I had better "cowboy up" and get ready for my second bull. The truth is I should have never gotten on my second bull. I know that now, but at the time, I didn't see any issue with it. Besides, it was "just a little knock on the head; nothing serious." So when the last section approached, I grabbed my bull rope and headed down the tunnel to the bucking chutes.

When incurring a concussion, your reflexes are usually delayed. Bull riding is very dependent on reflexes and muscle memory. A bull rider relies on his body to automatically make the moves he has taught himself to anticipate, through hundreds of hours of ground work on a stationary barrel or horseback and training in the practice pen. When his reflexes are delayed, his movements are delayed. When his movements are delayed, he gets behind. When he is behind, he is now chasing where he needs to be rather than already being there. This can open a bull rider up to a potentially painful buckoff.

That is exactly what happened to me in this instance. I was behind from the first jump out of the gate. This bull was getting a lot of air, spinning into my hand, and I was sitting just outside of the "pocket" to the right; away from my riding hand and away from his spin. With each jump, I would get a little more behind until I found myself sitting back on my pockets and on the end of my riding arm. With how high this bull was jumping, and the power he had in his kicking motion, this was a very bad combination. I want to be sitting *up* on my legs when a bull begins his jump forward – not sitting down on his back but rather a gap between myself and his back – with my shoulders over his shoulders to take the power away. Since I was out of shape on the end of my arm, leaned back instead of "floating" over his front end, when the bull started his jump that put me at the discretion of his full power.

I may not remember what knocked me out the first time that day, but there is no doubt what knocked me out the second time. When the bull kicked, it acted like a slingshot, shooting me forward. As I was moving forward, his front end was now coming back up to start the next jump, colliding two moving forces between my facemask and his head. It was such a hard impact that my helmet cut a straight line across my forehead where the outside of the helmet pushed through the padding and against my skin. There was no doubt I was knocked out this time. I immediately went into a fencing position as I came crashing back to the ground.

I don't remember anything once our heads met. They said I eventually woke up in the arena and even walked off under my own power with the assistance of the medical staff on hand. My next true memory was in the locker room, sitting against the wall next to my gear bag, with a paramedic cleaning the dirt and blood from my face. I figured my night was over and I could relax.

But then I found out I still had one more bull to ride. Less than ten guys rode both of their bulls; which meant the rest of the spots for the short go were filled by the highest scores on one bull ridden. I ended up with one of the highest scores in the first round, and that score was more than enough to get me into the short round. The biggest problem with this is I now had only around twenty minutes from when I woke up in the arena until I had to mount my third bull of the night.

Once again, remember that head injuries were not at the forefront of concerns during this time. Broken bones rarely prevented someone from riding another bull. So, how would getting knocked out be any different? Besides, I thought it would make a good story to laugh about with my friends later. In the end it *has* made a good story to laugh about, but I wouldn't recommend living it out in real life.

I don't remember much of the next fifteen minutes. I have bits and pieces once again scattered throughout my memory. I recall someone else had to put my rope on my bull for me. Later, my friends told me I actually started to climb down on the wrong bull thinking it was mine. They had to persuade me, emphatically, that my bull was actually two chutes down. I don't remember this but they sure do and, once again, it makes for a good story.

When I finally got on the right bull, my friend, who was pulling my rope, had to lay the tail of the rope across my hand before my instinct finally kicked in to take my wrap myself and slide up onto my rope. I was completely oblivious and merely going through the motions. I do remember hearing the announcer hyping the crowd with, "*Less than 30 minutes ago, we saw Nick laying motionless in the arena! Now he's already getting back on! Make some noise for this tough cowboy!*" The truth was, I was in no shape to be getting on a bull, especially one of that caliber.

Looking back, my friends admit they should have seen the warning signs, stepped in, and not let me get on that last bull. But that's always a hard thing to do: telling a friend to stop what they're doing because you know it's not good for them or has potentially life-altering harm. It's easy to say, in retrospect, what we *could* have done or what we *should* have said. But the reality is, it was in the past and is out of our hands now. All we can do moving forward is learn from the past and try to prevent something like this in the future.

If you are in a sport of any kind and see a friend trying to compete shortly after being seriously knocked out, I implore you, no *I beg you*, step in. Be the friend who stops a bad situation from turning worse. They may not appreciate it at the time. They may get mad at you. They may even hate you for it. They, quite possibly, could go through life never realizing what that one thing you did will mean for their long-term health. But I have learned by now that I would much rather be the friend who speaks up, despite ridicule or persecution, than the friend who blames himself for someone else's injury because I didn't have the guts to step in and stop it. I've had that conversation with friends from that day, and I had to reassure them that it was ultimately my decision, not theirs. Would I have listened to them had they tried to stop me? I honestly can't answer that question with a "yes" or a "no". I would like to say I would have. But I also know myself, and I know that giving up or stopping are not in my DNA. Besides, I had been knocked out twice already that night. What's the worst that could happen? It turns out, far worse could happen.

Getting jerked down onto the bull's head, two jumps into the ride, was the last thing I remember. My next memory was the morning after, waking up in the camper on the back of our rodeo-rig, not knowing where I was. It was like I was crashing towards his head, blinked, and was in the camper. I climbed out of the camper and realized we were parked at the location of our next rodeo. The brightness of the sun hitting my face made me feel like I was going to puke my guts out where I was standing. I walked around until I found my traveling partner, who was in the contestant hospitality tent eating lunch. I apologized to him that he had to make the entire drive through the night by himself; thinking I must have slept the whole drive. That's when I found out the scariest part of this whole story: I drove the entire 10+ hours through the night and still, to this day, don't remember any of it. Like I said: good story to laugh about later, not something I would recommend living out in real life.

Rewind to what everyone else remembers that I don't. As I'm sure you have guessed by now, I got knocked out pretty bad on my third bull. Real bad. Everyone said I was a *blast* to hang around in the locker room afterwards, though. They said I kept repeating the same sentences over and over again, asking the same questions, and having the same shocked reaction whenever they would answer them. One friend told me, later, that he ended up hanging around me the rest of the night, because he noticed when people were being nice by offering a Tylenol, ibuprofen, or aspirin, I would keep accepting them; not remembering any of the pills I had already taken. So he would stop people and kindly say, "Thank you. He already had some." That is what good friends are for. Truthfully I think he was hanging around more for the entertainment factor; also what good friends are for.

When it was time to leave, I was apparently adamant that I drive since the orders from the doctor at the event were that I stay awake for the next twelve hours. My traveling partner said I talked the whole way, which if you know me that probably wasn't too far out of the ordinary. What was out of the ordinary, though, was that I wasn't making any sense when I spoke. Eventually, we got to our destination – to this day, I still don't know how – and I climbed into the camper to get some sleep.

By the time the rodeo started that evening, I was back to riding bulls as if nothing had happened. I may have felt like I had been run over by a Mack Truck, but "the show must go on, and the bills must get paid."

I didn't think it had that big of an effect on me until I got back to college the next week. I teased earlier that I wasn't that smart, but the reality is actually the opposite; especially when it came to math. My freshman year of college, in 2000, one of my math professors convinced me to get my IQ tested. My IQ was designated a score of 148. My neurologist told me he is convinced that my high IQ, before all of the concussions, is one of the biggest reasons why I am so high-functioning today, despite the severity of the injury to my brain.

For evaluation purposes, I went through the IQ testing process again during the "period of discovery" in 2009 which I will be discussing in chapter 10. Surprisingly it had only dropped five points to a 143. This is highly intriguing to me. I thought my many struggles to retain knowledge now, as opposed to when I first had my IQ tested, would have meant that I would drop at least 30 points. That's not the case. While I may struggle with motor skills and retaining knowledge, the base of my IQ is still mostly intact. I believe it is the biggest contributing factor to me being able to articulate my struggles.

After graduating high school when I was seventeen years old, I immediately pursued a collegiate career. I was motivated to graduate college early, while attaining a high GPA in the process. So I worked hard to make sure I maintained high grades while balancing a heavier workload of classes; all while still rodeoing full time. Up until the night I got knocked out three times, everything was going as planned. When I came back to school from this specific run of rodeos, however, everything was different. I would go to class and be confused when the professor talked. I couldn't follow along, as everything they were saying seemed like gibberish to me. I was now failing tests, something I had never had happen in my life. The hardest thing to swallow was when I started failing the actual classes themselves. Overnight, I went from being a mainstay on the President's List every semester to getting failing grades. How was this happening to me? How could I not understand what is being taught or retain what I am learning? None of it made sense. I felt ashamed. I didn't want people to think of me as a failure.

It wasn't until years later I realized this decline in academic skills was due to too many repetitive blows to my head. Three concussions in one night may not have been the start of my problems, but they were definitely the start to my cognitive decline.

Things that used to be easy were now becoming hard as a result. After failing the same advanced classes over and over again, I went from my dream of graduating with a degree in Corporate Business Management with a near-perfect GPA, to now having to drop out of college just 12 credit hours short of my degree. In my mind, at the time, it made me think I was nothing more than a massive failure. One more big blow of feeling like a failure, a year and a half later, would be all my brain needed to "take me over the edge."

Chapter 7

Sudden End to a Rodeo Dream

Nick (18) aboard Shag McNasty of Rumford Rodeo Company in the short round at the Cornhusker Stampede College Rodeo in Lincoln, NE. Photo Courtesy of JJJ Photography

I wanted nothing more than to be a Professional Bull Rider for an entire career. I had it all planned out in my head. I was going to retire from riding when I was in my late thirties. I would then pursue my other occupational goals of either working in business on the corporate level or becoming a sports broadcaster, preferably for rodeo. But first I needed to fulfill my dream of a full and satisfying bull riding career. I knew I had the talent to "hang with the big boys". I just needed to stay healthy. I didn't expect those dreams to also be crushed – and my bull riding career to be over – a few weeks before my 22nd birthday.

Rodeo is a rare sport where you can pursue multiple levels of competition simultaneously. You can be considered a professional, even at the highest levels, and still compete at a collegiate level. This is not true in any other sport I know of. Because of this, I was able to ride at the collegiate level, while attending college on a rodeo scholarship, and still pursue my professional dreams part time on the side as my collegiate vocation progressed.

My problem wasn't that I couldn't compete at those levels. My problem was that I couldn't stay healthy. Actually, my problem was that I wouldn't let myself *get* healthy. Every time I gained momentum, I would get hurt again. After my neck healed from the injury talked about in an earlier chapter, I was riddled with a bevy of injuries over the next couple of years. Dislocated shoulders, a broken tailbone twice, multiple broken ribs, broken fingers, and torn groin muscles were normal wear and tear of the sport.

When I dropped out of college, I could now pursue a professional career full time. Everything was looking positive with my rodeo dreams. Something "clicked" for that next level, and I was now riding better than I ever had in my life. I was getting to travel with some of my childhood rodeo heroes and compete against the best bulls and bull riders in the world. I was barely 20 years old. I felt like my bull riding was reaching new levels. My dream was finally becoming a reality. But once that momentum started rolling, the injury bug struck again.

I don't even remember exactly where I was when this happened … somewhere down south. I had drawn a big, tall Brahman bull, which I always loved getting on because their style of bucking fit my taller frame of body. During the process of dismounting my bull after the buzzer, my spur hung in my bull rope while the bull was in what is called a "belly roll". Since the bull was rolling to the same side I got off on, when my spur hung, the slight pull on the bull's side caused him to flip onto his side, pulling him down onto my back. The impact broke the T-10 and T-11 vertebrae in my back. I had a temporary scare as I initially couldn't feel my legs. But thankfully it was just a stinger and I got feeling back while riding in the ambulance. I went home for a few weeks to help my dad around the ranch and let it heal. As soon as I could move without losing my breath, which took a couple months, I strapped a brace around my torso that held my back in place and went back to riding bulls.

It didn't take long before I was winning money consistently again. The period after my broken back I saw another increase in my riding abilities after I had the opportunity to consistently get on the caliber of bulls that were being hauled to the PBRs where I was competing. I felt like I was improving exponentially every year, but the increase this particular year seemed like the biggest to date. Most bull riders reach their peak in their mid-to-late-twenties. So, to be feeling this large of a jump in my riding abilities when I was 20 years old, my confidence was burgeoning quickly.

I had been having issues with my free arm dislocating. It had dislocated so many times it was now going in and out of socket on a regular basis. On two different occasions, it dislocated while I was still on the back of a bull. The first time it happened, it caught me off guard. So, I jumped off, landing on my feet, trying to protect the shoulder. The second time it happened the bull was spinning into my hand. Since the only direction to safely get off of a bull without risking getting hung up in your rope is into your hand, I had no choice but to suck my elbow to my side the best I could and tough it out for a paycheck. It was a weird sensation feeling the shoulder ball swing back and forth inside my arm as the bull bucked. I finally decided to try wearing a neoprene brace to see if it would hold the shoulder in place better. After trying it on a few bulls in the practice pen, it felt great.

One of my first events wearing the brace was at a PBR event in Springfield, Missouri. I had a really good bull drawn that was known for having a lot of centrifugal force if you let him get you outside of the spin. He was spinning to the left, into my riding hand. I had a really good inside hold with my left leg and he was packing me around the corner. I decided to get cocky and try to spur him for a few extra points. Big mistake.

Older bulls like him are smart and usually have a trick or two up their sleeve. He was setting me up. As soon as I pulled my outside foot, he kicked into another gear, spinning faster. That pulled me a little to the outside. Learning from my mistake when I cracked the C-2 vertebrae in my neck, I disregarded my dislocation issues and made the necessary move where I cut the corner by throwing my free arm behind my head instead of over my head. A combination of his centrifugal force, the neoprene brace putting pressure on my shoulder, and the angle I threw my arm sucked my shoulder out of socket and hurled me to the ground immediately, spinning me sideways as I descended. I landed directly on my elbow, jamming the ball of the dislocated arm into the side of the shoulder socket. This started a long night full of extreme pain at the Springfield hospital's emergency room. Pro rodeo legend Dr. Tandy Freeman performed surgery a few weeks later in Dallas, Texas, to fix the damage.

Around that same time, I met a girl from Deming, New Mexico, named Ivy Wilkin. I used the recovery period from my surgery as an opportunity to get to know her better. During that time I fell madly in love with her. After completing my rehab, I made up my mind that I wanted to marry this girl. What a better time to propose than at my first PBR event back from this injury? It was in Gallup, New Mexico, only a few hours from her hometown. I could spend some time visiting her leading up to the event, then have her parents come up to Gallup and my parents come down to New Mexico for the full weekend of the PBR event. I had it all planned out. I was going to ask her dad's permission at dinner our first night in Gallup after the first round of the event. Then I was going to ask her hand in marriage before the second round started the next night. It was the perfect plan. Plus it would all happen while I was re-launching my bull riding career after a grueling nine months of physical rehab. Life couldn't be better.

Two days before the bull riding event, Ivy and I decided to go to Elephant Butte Lake with some of her friends to waterski. While driving to the lake, Ivy momentarily reached for a hair clip. Just a second of taking her eyes off the road was all it took. The interstate turned and she didn't. As she tried to recover, we hit some sagebrush alongside the interstate causing her small Ford Ranger to turn fully sideways and flip on a dime. A combination of the top-heaviness of the truck, the steep downhill grade of the road in that section, and how quickly we turned sideways sent us into a scary wreck. According to the officer on the scene the truck rolled six and a half times. We came to rest with the truck lying on its passenger side. I was knocked out, with my head laying on the pavement after the window beside me had busted out from the crash. Ivy was hanging from her seatbelt. The blood dripping from her nose onto my face brought me back to consciousness. Other people traveling on the interstate that day began helping us out of the truck, which had now caught on fire.

This is the type of crash people never walk away from. In fact, one of Ivy's best childhood friends, Cassie, was killed in a car crash at the same exact location around two years later. I can't tell you why we walked away and Cassie didn't. It always breaks my heart for her parents and sister, who we are still good friends with to this day.

Ivy and I were rushed to the nearest emergency room in Las Cruces, New Mexico, where the medical team expected us both to arrive with major injuries. But, as evidenced so many times in my life, God had his hand over us; not only during the crash but also on the 40 minute drive to the hospital. We were both released later that night with minor injuries. Ivy walked away highly shaken, but relatively unscathed other than some scrapes, cuts, and bruises. I had a severe concussion, a cut on the side of my forehead from either the window or the pavement, and little shards of glass stuck throughout the rest of my body. In fact, three years later, I pulled a small piece of glass out from under the skin in my forehead. Then, almost ten years later I pulled a piece of glass out of my index fingertip. I can feel a smaller piece of glass still embedded deep in that finger today.

Two days after the accident, I was pretty sore from head to toe. I shouldn't have gotten on any bulls that close to such a bad wreck. I had a full medical release to be able to withdraw from the event without any fines. Nobody would have questioned it. But I couldn't wait any longer. I had just sat out nine months recovering from surgery and rehabbing my shoulder. I couldn't let any more time pass if I wanted to make a run at qualifying to the PBR World Finals. Plus I had planned out this entire weekend to propose to my girlfriend. I wasn't going to let some car wreck ruin my perfect night. But, as it turned out, I never got the chance to propose to Ivy that weekend, or even ask her dad's permission.

With yet another concussion, my reflexes were even slower than before. I drew a rank little four-year-old bull named Here Kitty Kitty. This was only the second or third time he was hauled to a professional bull riding, so there wasn't a very long scouting report on him yet. One of my rodeo heroes, Adriano Moraes – who I had become pretty good friends with by this point – had drawn him the weekend before and bucked off of him.

On that trip, the bull was in the latch to the left and beat Adriano around the corner, making him have to play catch-up, and eventually throwing the Brazilian off. Since Adriano is considered one of the best bull riders in *history*, with multiple World Championship Titles to his credit, I knew I had my hands full with this young bull. As Adriano was pulling my bull rope that night, I remember he kept telling me, "You have to get around that corner, Nick. Get around that corner! You need to already be there because it's going to come fast!"

Usually in bull riding, a rider rides a bull jump for jump; meaning they never expect the bull to do the same thing each jump, or to have the same exact trip every time. Every jump is a new jump. Yes, the bull could repeat the same jump or have the same trip fifty times in a row, but you can never *expect* that. A bull can switch things up on a dime. These are extremely intelligent animals. We are talking about an animal that can feel a tiny individual fly land on his back and twitch the muscle exactly where that fly is to shake him off. He can feel exactly where the rider is at all times.

The 8-second ride can become as much a chess-match between the rider and bull as it is a battle of attrition and athleticism. Smart bulls will try strategies to get the rider out of shape and gain an advantage. They may hop and skip a jump, in an attempt to get the rider's timing off. They may scoot forward a jump without kicking, in an attempt to rock the rider back onto his pockets, taking the center of gravity off of the rider's hips and legs where he wants it. They may belly roll in an attempt to get the rider's hips out of position and rock his momentum to one side or the other. They may fade into a spin then fade *away* from the spin, swapping between centrifugal and centripetal force on the rider's body. They may switch directions hoping to catch the rider in a position where he is recovering from a previous jump and can't make that transition with them. The reality is these bulls are extremely intelligent and know exactly what their job is: to buck their rider off. Just writing about this gets my adrenaline pumping and cravings stirred. I would love nothing more than to still be able to get on a bull that is spinning to the left, fading to the left, and backing up into me. Give me a few minutes while I sit here and daydream…

So the truth is a bull rider can't go into a ride expecting anything other than to execute the fundamentals every jump. These are animals. And while they may be habitual, they are extremely unpredictable. A rider wants to start every jump the same way. When that bull's front end comes up, the rider goes back to "home base" – his shoulders squared over the bull's shoulders, back straight, free arm reaching forward, lifting his butt off the bull's back, keeping his hips square with his shoulders, and putting the pressure on his knees so whenever the bull moves a direction the rider's legs pack the rider into that corner. This is ideal for when the rider is in total control.

But there are instances when the rider's body gets out of shape and he has to play catch-up. The rider must still go back to "home base" as the bull begins his jump, but then uses the crest of the jump to adjust his position, trying to get himself as close to back into the "pocket" as he can. It boils down to how quickly the rider can get himself back into control. The jump when a rider bucks off is rarely the jump that bucked him off. It is usually three to four jumps earlier, when he got out of shape and wasn't able to get back into position.

If a bull is known to have a specific move, or a tough corner to get around, the rider can "set a trap". This is where he already starts moving his hips, shoulders, and body into that direction in anticipation of that move. This is a high risk, high reward technique, because the rider is selling himself out in expectation of the bull making that move. That bull can feel, in the rider's legs, what moves he is expecting, and if the rider shows his hand too quickly the bull could decide to switch directions on a dime. The more experienced a bull, the harder it is to set a trap on them.

Some bulls don't care. They know they are rank and don't need to pull any tricks to succeed. At the same time the rider knows the only way to make every corner is to throw everything they have at that corner's momentum. These matchups make for the best, and most fun, bull rides, as you can see the rider and bull both throwing caution to the wind every jump. For an example of this, look up and watch videos of Jose Vitor Leme on Woopaa or Cassio Dias on Manhater.

I rarely set traps for bulls. But if the bull I drew beat Adriano Moraes around the corner, then I knew it had to be a pretty hard corner to get around. Plus this bull was young, and it is usually easier to get away with setting traps on younger bulls because they may not have the experience to recognize a trap yet. I miscalculated how smart this little bull was.

He blew out of the chute and started to turn back to the left immediately. As he jumped out, I set a hard trap to the left anticipating that corner, but he felt my body starting to move that direction. As soon as his left foot hit the ground, he immediately switched directions, ducking back around and spinning the other way. My reflexes were way behind, all of my momentum was moving left, and he was moving right. It's safe to say I didn't make that corner to the right. He threw me off in style, but at least I was thrown away from him.

Before the event, I was wondering why they called him Here Kitty Kitty. As he turned and came at me faster than I could get to my feet, my literal thought was "Ahhh. Here Kitty Kitty! I get it now!" He ran me clean over. Before I could get rolled over onto my knees to get back up, he had already turned around and was coming back for seconds. I then proceeded to receive one of the worst hookings of my career. The bull fighters tried everything they could to get him off of me, but he was focused on only one thing: me. Every time I could get my legs between me and him to push open a little gap between us, he would be right back on top of me as soon as that gap opened. No matter what the bull fighters did, he wouldn't take his focus off of me. He was simply too fast for me to be able to get out of there.

In the process of this hooking, he stepped on my left arm in-between the shoulder and elbow, dislocating that shoulder laterally. A few seconds later, he stepped on the arm again, causing even more damage. When he finally wore out and the bullfighters were able to get him away from me, I couldn't feel my left arm and was in full shock. I seriously thought my arm had been ripped from my body since I couldn't feel it or see it. But the arm was bent behind me and out of my peripheral vision. I was able to get to my feet and at least run to the chutes. I was ushered into an ambulance and off we went. Instead of proposing to my girlfriend as I planned, I was now being life-flighted to Albuquerque, New Mexico, because Gallup didn't have the facilities to repair my arm correctly.

This is when the discouragement set in. It was literally *one* professional event after being out for nine months with a major shoulder surgery. Yet, here we are again, but with the *other* shoulder, and this one in seemingly worse shape. I took a step back and re-evaluated everything. Do I want to make another grueling attempt at rehab to pursue my career, or was the volume of injuries too much to handle at this point? Do I want to keep putting my body through this, facing continual frustrations, or was I just letting my frustration in the moment dictate my future? Whatever my decision was going to be – hang up my rope or come back stronger – I was prepared to fully commit to that decision.

I didn't get to propose to Ivy in New Mexico. It wasn't until a month later at the ranch in South Dakota, surrounded by a herd of bucking horses, with the sun setting over the horizon of the Badlands, that I finally found the perfect moment to ask. She, of course, said "yes".

The following week, Ivy accompanied me to Gillette, Wyoming, where I was instructing the bull riding at a rodeo bible camp, and she volunteered as a counselor for the girls at that camp. During this trip, I knew we could discuss my bull riding future together, as Ivy's future would now be tied to mine. I was confident I would make a decision one way or another while there, and Ivy assured me she would fully support whatever decision I made.

The camp was being held at CAM-PLEX, the same facilities where the National High School Finals Rodeo are held, and in the same arena I was first introduced to the sport of rodeo as a little kid. During that camp, being in that arena, made me reflect back on the entirety of my career. I made the decision that I would forever regret not giving it my all, and riding bulls was something I still wanted to do. Not only that, I was more determined than I had ever been to pursue that dream. The more I thought about it, the more excited I got for the possibilities of the future.

The following weekend, on my way home from that camp, I received a crushing punch to the gut. I had just dropped Ivy off at the airport in Rapid City, South Dakota, and was pointing my car down Highway 44 back to the ranch, when my phone rang.

As a bull rider, this is the phone call you never want to get. I had numerous doctors in the past tell me not to ride bulls anymore, but I also knew they were speaking out of concern for my health. It wasn't that I truly couldn't ride bulls anymore; it was that they didn't want to see me keep getting hurt. Only one doctor on the planet, Dr. Tandy Freeman, had earned my respect so much that if he told me it was over, it would be over. Tandy was the doctor for all the top rodeo athletes in both the PBR and PRCA. He had already done the surgery for my right arm and was looking over the medical reports to do surgery on my left arm. I was hoping he was calling to schedule an appointment for the next surgery. Instead, he told me some of the worst news I had heard to date.

Paraphrased to the best of my remembrance, he said, "Nick. Due to the angle of the injury, with it being laterally dislocated, it will be a tough fix to keep it from pulling out again when lifting on your rope. I can put a temporary fix on it. But eventually that will no longer hold, and you risk doing irreparable damage to that arm if it dislocates with your hand still in the rope. If I hadn't just fixed your other shoulder, I would tell you to switch riding hands. But neither will be able to handle that level of torque over time. I think it's time you started looking for a new career."

This was devastating. My whole life's dream was gone in an instant. I went from what should have been the best time of my life – a new fiance, a revived passion to pursue the bull riding dream – to what felt like the worst day in my life. That drive home was brutal. I started thinking about things I had never thought about before. My mind didn't go to "what's next?" My mind went to "it's over." Why was I having these thoughts? I've never contemplated suicide before. It's never even been an afterthought. But now it was all I could think about. I failed as a bull rider *and* at college. I was telling myself I had no future, therefore, I had failed in life and failed everyone who believed in me. It wasn't until later in life I would learn how closely these thoughts would be tied to my concussions.

Many turns of the road, I would speed up knowing my car couldn't make the next corner, only to come to my senses and slow down at the last second. One section of that stretch of Highway 44 winds back and forth through a series of Badlands walls. Through tears, I fought back every urge to speed my car off the road and into one of those Badlands cliffs.

I didn't know what was happening to me. Could it be just because of failure that I wanted to do this to myself? There has to be more! I drove through the small town of Interior and pulled over to the side of the road, just beyond the turn into what used to be Woodenknife Cafe, and the birthplace of the famous Woodenknife Indian Fry Bread Mix. I climbed out, walked to the bar ditch, sat down, and cried. I don't know how long I sat there with my head in my hand. It could have been minutes. It could have been hours. But I eventually recovered from my pity, got in my car, and drove to the ranch. I didn't say a word to anyone and acted like nothing had happened.

That didn't stop the emotion over the next few months, maybe even years. I was mad. I was selfish. I knew what I wanted, but I couldn't have it. If I couldn't have it, then I surely didn't want to watch my friends get it. That's when I let the worst emotion I could develop. I became bitter.

Chapter 8

Bitter or Better

Nick (35) and his brother, Nate (37), on the Red Carpet at the 2017 ProRodeo Hall of Fame Gold Buckle Gala, at the South Point Casino and Resort in Las Vegas, Nevada

Bitterness is a dangerous emotion to let fester in your heart. Once it takes root, it grows to the point of consuming every other emotion that person has. They become bitter at their circumstances. Bitter at the world. Bitter at anyone whose dreams are not as crushed as theirs. They become bitter at any of their friends or coworkers who are succeeding. They regress into the recesses of their sorrow, and lose sight of anything outside their own pity.

Most people don't even recognize when they are living in bitterness. They go through life telling themself they are fine despite their circumstance; that they are supportive of everything their friends, family, and coworkers are accomplishing. But then they let the negative thoughts rule their feelings whenever they see someone else outperform their efforts, or when they don't receive the recognition they feel they deserve. Bitterness clouds their perception and skews their adaptation to the resulting offense.

I can speak to this with experience because I was once consumed in that bitterness myself. I have also learned from the mistakes that allowed bitterness to encompass every corner of my mind. Looking back, I can trace how small bitterness slowly grew to a heart besieged by it. It all starts in the mind. If you find yourself living in bitterness, the only way to dig yourself out is to control your mentality. Control the way you think. Control the *attitude* of your mind.

How you perceive something directly affects how you process it. Let me give you some examples I've learned that help *me* control *my* mentality in these circumstances. None of these are natural responses. Every single one I have to *consciously* make the effort to rewire my perception, so as to not taint my processing of the situation. Whenever I *do* perceive it in offense, out of my more natural response, I have to go back and take those previous thoughts captive to change my focus. This takes honest self-evaluation, completely devoid of personal pride. For example:

- Instead of seeing what someone says negatively about me as criticism or an "attack," I try to see it as shining a light on an area I may need to improve on. Is what they criticized me for an issue I need to address or something they are simply saying out of their own bitterness? Is that something I need to work on? What steps do I need to take to improve in those areas?

- Instead of seeing failure, I try to see it as a learning opportunity. I tried and I failed. But at least I tried. What can I learn from it? Rather than focusing on the failure itself, I try to divert my focus to what I did right, what I did wrong, and what areas I can improve on to lessen the chances of failure next time.

- Instead of seeing someone else's newfound opportunity as "they were just lucky to be in the right place at the right time," I try to see it as hustling to put themself in the correct place to be there when that opportunity finally presented itself. What do I need to do to have myself positioned for the next opportunity? *Opportunity looks a whole lot like hard work.*

- Instead of seeing a minute task as "wasted time", I try to see it as "you never know who is watching." Am I truthfully putting my best effort into this task? If I can be trusted with little, I can be trusted with much. What is my attitude towards this minute task saying about my passion to do more? Championships are won in the details. Cutting corners or blowing off "easy work" now will only hinder my execution of the details during larger tasks in the future.

- Instead of seeing an opportunity to put someone else down to make myself feel better about my shortcomings compared to theirs, I try to see it as an opportunity to learn from someone doing something better than I am. Attempting to drag someone else down to my level is more destructive to me than it is to them. What do *I* need to do to elevate myself to *their* level? What areas are they beating me in? Change it from an attitude of jealousy to an attitude of admiration.

- Instead of looking at someone else and thinking to myself, "I wish I had what they have," I try to envision how much work that person put in, that nobody else saw or will even appreciate, to get to the level they are now. I only see the end result. I don't see the work it took to get there. Am I willing to put that kind of work in myself? Am I willing to push through procrastination? Am I willing to still work hard on days when my mind is trying to convince me "it's okay to cut corners, nobody is watching"?

It is all in how you let your mind perceive and process the situation in front of you. In each of these instances, one mindset is viewed through the eyes of bitterness, while the other is through the eyes of self-improvement.

I've learned that now, but I wasn't always that way. When facing the reality of my bull riding career being over, I was slowly letting that bitterness have complete control over my emotions. It wasn't until a statement from my brother, Nate, a few years after my injury, that changed my entire perspective on my circumstance. "*You can get bitter. Or you can get better. But you can't be both.*"

Here I was feeling sorry for myself, consumed by what I thought was a life-crushing turn of events. Yet, the whole time I have a brother who has been living in a far worse situation than me. I at least got to *taste* the professional rodeo dream. His professional dream was lost as quickly as it started.

Nate was eighteen years old during his senior year in high school, which meant even though he was still competing at the high school rodeo level, he could also compete professionally. As soon as Nate turned eighteen, he purchased his PRCA Permit. There was an extraordinarily talented group of saddle bronc riders in our circle of friends in South Dakota high school rodeo at that time. Many of them went on to have very successful professional careers. It was as woofy of a roster of high school competitors as it could get. Future PRCA superstars like JJ Elshere, Chad Ferley, Ryan Elshere, Jesse Bail, and Jeff Willert are barely skimming the surface of the talented high school bronc riders in our region of South Dakota during this period. Not only could my brother compete with them, he was considered one of the best in that group.

After a good start to their early professional career, Nate and one of his best friends, Jesse Bail, entered a wave of pro rodeos starting in May of 1998. They were going to hit the road for the summer to accomplish the professional rodeo dream together. Nate had broken his leg a few months earlier from jumping off a bucking horse in the practice pen and his leg landing awkwardly on a divot in the arena dirt. As soon as the doctor cut the cast off, Nate was back to riding bucking horses.

The first weekend of May, we had a grouping of high school rodeos in Kadoka, White River, and Burke, called The Triple Crown, that kicks off the South Dakota high school rodeo season every year. It was during this set of rodeos, one year earlier, that the four-wheeler story I told earlier in the book happened. We only lived 45 miles away from Kadoka. So, our house was usually the place everyone stayed in-between Kadoka and White River's rodeos. We bucked a bunch of horses and bulls in the practice pen at our house in the days leading up to the Triple Crown, so a bunch of our friends were already crashing at our place. We had dozens of roughstock cowboys in sleeping bags scattered across the floors of our house that weekend.

This set of high school rodeos would be a good test on Nate's leg – despite being cleared to ride, he was still relegated to crutches during the final stages of healing – before he and Jesse left from Burke for their string of professional rodeos over the next few months. He did well in Kadoka – I think maybe even winning it, or placing second, if I remember right – and the leg felt good.

That night, back at our place, was like most nights with this group of cowboys; filled with laughter and pranks on each other that lasted well into the night. At the moment, you don't realize you are living through a night that will become a core memory amongst everyone in that group. What we didn't know, at the time, was that it would be the last night with my brother, who was a central component of our large group, before he broke his neck.

In the morning, our caravan of cars, trucks, and vans full of rodeo cowboys, headed to White River, South Dakota.

May 2nd, 1998. A date that will forever ring in my memory.

I was riding to the rodeo in the Brewer brothers' van, our favorite rodeo rig of choice at that time, with my brother, the Brewers, and a few others. Those not driving, or riding shotgun, typically played cards on a table in the back of their van. You have to understand the relationship between my brother and me. We were and still are extremely close. He has always been, and always will be my best friend. Our entire childhood, and even into adulthood, we have gone through life with people confusing which of us is Nick and which of us is Nate. It happens so often, we joke that my nickname is "Nate" and his is "Nick." But like any brothers who spend almost every hour around each other, we also fought a lot. Not just with words. We were both pretty scrappy back in the day. So during this van ride, we got into an argument over something stupid during the card game, I can't even remember what – probably him cheating at the card game because he was always good at getting away with cheating at cards. I just remember I was mad at my brother. I was the young one in the van, a sophomore in a van full of juniors and seniors, so I probably even sat in the back immaturely, pouting the rest of the drive.

At the rodeo, games of hacky sack were very popular to pass the extremely long periods of time the timed events would take up during a high school rodeo. I was so mad at my brother, for whatever idiotic or trivial thing at that moment, I remember I didn't even play hacky sack with the boys like usual.

When the bronc riding came around, I helped my brother like always. I would help him with his saddle bronc horses, and he always pulled my rope for my bulls. That didn't change the fact that I was still mad at him, and was being immature about it. So, even though I was helping him, we didn't talk the whole time.

When Nate nodded his head, and marked the horse out on the first jump, he felt his leg hit the end of the stirrup and something didn't feel right. Rather than hurt the leg again at a high school rodeo, he decided to bail off. What all transpired next occurred in a split-second, but somehow seemed to happen in slow motion. As Nate was jumping off, he tried to tuck to prevent from landing on the leg again. Unfortunately, at the same time, the horse ducked in the direction he was bailing off. Now, instead of going off the side of the horse, he went directly over the horse's head. As she started her next jump, and her head was coming up during that motion, it flipped his body over her head. He was now upside down, under her head, with his legs on each side of her neck, in what was turning into the perfect storm. When she started her kicking motion, the motion of her head coming down with the kick drove Nate's forehead into the ground. The momentum of the horse kept Nate's body moving forward, bending him like a scorpion so acutely, the back of his head touched his tailbone. The motion of him being driven into the ground under the horse's head looked extremely similar to those "nodding donkey" oil pumpjacks you see scattered all over the countryside.

When the dust settled, I saw Nate still laying on the ground where he landed. I immediately knew something wasn't right. I bailed over the chute and ran out to him. As soon as I got beside him he said, "I can't move my legs." Soon more cowboys began gathering at his side. The entire place fell silent as the echoes of something serious happening in the arena started to reach every corner of the facility. By the time the EMTs were loading Nate into the back of the ambulance, the arena had now turned into a scene filled with hundreds of high school rodeo athletes and their parents gathered around the ambulance, kneeling on one knee, hat in hand, praying.

Even now, thinking back at this time, it is the most emotional I have found myself while writing this book. Tears are streaming down my face as I type. I blame the side effect of increased emotional response due to all of the concussions for this reaction. The truth is, that's just how much my brother truly means to me.

My mom hopped into the ambulance with Nate, and they took off screaming towards the closest hospital, which was over an hour away in Pierre. Friends told us they would gather up Nate's and my rodeo equipment for us, so my dad and I could jump into his truck to follow the ambulance without having to worry about anything else. Getting on my bull later that day wasn't even a thought. The only thing on my mind was getting to my brother and making sure he was okay.

Every time I rode in that arena after that day was always emotional for me. I had a "ride for Nate" mentality where, buck off or ride, I was committed to spurring my bull as soon as the gate opened. Of all of the rodeos and bull ridings I had won over the years, winning the bull riding at White River's high school rodeo, both of my junior and senior years, were two of my most emotional wins. In a total act of chance, all three rodeos I won in that arena – the two high school rodeos and a SDRA rodeo – I came out of the same exact chute my brother did his last ride.

The ambulance beat my dad and me to the hospital by about fifteen minutes. They had already loaded Nate onto a life-flight to Rapid City by the time we got there. So, we headed to the house to pack some clothes on our way to meet them in Rapid City. My dad is the toughest man I know. His nicknames of "Quigley" and "Captain Call," both after famous "tough guys" from western lore, are warranted. I've only seen my dad get emotional three times in my life. When my mom died from cancer, at the funeral of *his* mom only a few weeks after my mom's funeral, and on this drive.

All I could think about was how I had wasted all of that time at the rodeo being mad at my brother for something so trivial that I couldn't even remember what it was. I felt miserable. How inconsequential of a thing to be mad about in the grander scheme of life. The only thing on my mind was getting to my brother and telling him I was sorry.

When we got to the hospital, my dad met my mom and Nate in the intensive care unit, while I sat in the waiting room. As the hours passed, the waiting room filled with more and more of our rodeo friends and their families. When the rodeo ended, they all chose to drive to Rapid City to support Nate, which was hours of driving in the opposite direction of the rodeo in Burke the following day. So many people showed up, it got to the point that the waiting room was now standing room only. I remember a moment, when my mom had come out to give me an update, a nurse said to her, "This room is for family only." My mom just looked at her, while fighting back tears, and softly said, "Everyone here *is* family."

I stayed awake through the entire night, with my mom coming out to give me periodic updates before going back into their room. The X-rays on my brother's neck showed extensive damage. The doctors described it as if someone had set firecrackers exploding up and down his spine. One vertebra shattered so severely that when the swelling finally went down enough for surgery, it required 14 hours of surgery just to remove all of the broken pieces.

The night passed and I still had not been able to see my brother. The next day I was finally getting some sleep on a couch when my dad lightly shook me awake. "Your brother wants to see you."

I'll never forget walking into that room. The doctors needed to stretch his spine out, since it had collapsed so much during impact. My first view of Nate, after the accident, was him laying face down on the bed, his head shaved, with a metal rod drilled into each side of his head connected to a pulley system that was connected to weights hanging below him. He was wearing prism glasses that made it possible for him to watch the TV on the wall.

That day's NASCAR race was playing on the television. My brother didn't like racing, but my dad and I were huge fans. Nate never watched races with us. So, I honestly don't know if Nate was watching it that day because it was the channel the TV was stuck on, or if he had someone change the channel to the NASCAR race knowing I was going to be coming in to see him. I sat down in the chair beside his head, ready to tell him I was sorry for being mad at him the day before. But before I could get a word out my brother said, "I hope you know, I love you."

For one of the rarest moments in my life, I was speechless. Another word wasn't spoken between either of us.

We both just sat there in silence for hours, watching the race. Two brothers bonding even closer than before. I couldn't tell you very much about any of the thousands of races I've watched over the years. But this memory is so engrained into my mind that I know it was the NAPA 500 in Fontana, California, that day, and Mark Martin was the winner. I will never forget it.

While I am proud of my brother for many things, what I am most proud of is how he has rebounded through so many devastating events in his life, yet he still finds a way to remain positive. Broken necks and broken backs are a part of rodeo. A high percentage of roughstock rodeo athletes, at the professional level, will experience one or the other at least once in their career. Most escape without injury to their spine. Some don't. I have eight rodeo friends who are paralyzed, seven of them from rodeo accidents. Nate has impacted many of them, and helped them through some very tough times; much like Jerome Davis, a World Champion bull rider who broke his neck a few years before Nate, did for him. Similar to how I can relate to people with concussion issues, Nate can relate to rodeo athletes facing paralysis. If you aren't living *through* it, knowing the emotions and frustrations that accompany the situation, you truly can't speak *to* it.

Nate never let his accident define who he was. Rather than being known for the rest of his life as the kid who broke his neck at a high school rodeo, Nate has built such a successful life and career that most people, who have yet to meet him in person, are shocked when they see him in a wheelchair.

In the early 2000's, Nate was extremely forward-thinking about using a somewhat new technology, the internet, to advance the sport of rodeo. Before Nate started his business, if a local stock contractor wanted to sell his really good bucking bull to a professional stock contractor, he would have to haul that bull across the country to a live rodeo stock auction and hope the bull performed well enough at that event to sell. Before there was social media, or any ways to show a video online with websites like YouTube, Nate saw the potential of using the internet to connect rodeo stock breeders, scattered all over the country, to each other with online auctions. Not only that, but he had the foresight to give people with money an opportunity to invest into a bucking stock breeder with a dream. The Breeder's Connection was born.

The price of bucking bulls skyrocketed within a few years of Nate launching The Breeder's Connection. Owning bucking bulls was no longer just about hauling bulls to rodeos; it was now a sound money investment. As the popularity of owning stock in a bucking bull spread, Hollywood celebrities, musicians, businessmen, and professional athletes from numerous sports started investing their money into bucking bulls through Nate's website auctions. Actors, during popular movies, would make passing references about buying bucking bulls online; an on-screen nod to Nate's website. The Breeder's Connection quickly grew to being the premiere place to buy and sell some of the best bucking stock in the world.

While there are numerous websites copying Nate's vision today, The Breeders Connection was the first, and is still considered the most elite. Many in the rodeo industry consider Nate the "world's leading expert" when it comes to pricing and selling rodeo stock. The impact he has had on the sport of rodeo, and the stock contractor industry as a whole, is monumental.

His dream of riding at the NFR may have been lost, but Nate made it to the NFR in another way. The PRCA eventually hired Nate to produce the World Famous Benny Binion's NFR Bucking Horse and Bull Sale in Las Vegas, the most prestigious live rodeo stock auction in the world, held during the NFR every year. An NFR jacket, given to contestants and stock contractors who qualify to the NFR that year, is one of the most prestigious items a rodeo athlete can own. During Nate's first year of producing the NFR Sale, after the NFR Back Number Ceremony, he was surprised with his own NFR jacket. Nate now has a closet *full* of NFR jackets.

He accomplished *all* of this after his injury. He didn't let the injury define him. He let it fine tune him.

I have some friends who never recovered emotionally from a paralysis injury like my brother's. It breaks my heart to see this. But many other friends are extremely successful despite their paralysis. All of them faced extremely challenging moments. All of them hit a wall of the "feel-sorries" – anyone *not* in their shoes can't blame them for it, I surely don't. The difference between the ones who moved on to find success afterwards and the ones who didn't? The ones who moved on refused to stay surrounded by their challenge and pushed through their weakest moments.

I'll never forget getting the phone call from Shelby Vezain in 2018. Her husband, JR Vezain, was one of the top-ranked bareback riders in the world. I was living in the Houston, Texas, area at this time and JR was coming through for some pro rodeos. He and his traveling partners were going to stay at our house after their performance at the Pasadena PRCA Rodeo that night. I was at a wedding and planned to meet up with JR, who I consider one of my dearest friends, and his crew afterwards. That plan changed drastically when Shelby called. "JR's horse flipped over backwards on him. He said he felt his back snap, and he can't feel his legs. They are rushing him to Memorial Hermann in Houston. I'm going to fly down there. Can you please go be with him until I get there?"

I was already gone before we had even hung up the phone. My wife, my son, and I headed straight to

Memorial Hermann, where they had just taken JR back to Intensive Care. Tanner Aus and Anthony Thomas were already there as well. Since only two could be with him at a time, the three of us rotated turns going back there with him. Eventually, Richie and Paige Champion made it there too, after driving hours down from whatever rodeo Richie was riding at.

Shelby got stuck in a snowstorm in Montana, where they lived, and couldn't board a plane to Houston yet. After living through it with my brother, I knew how important it was to have someone there at all times, if anything just for Shelby's peace of mind. They moved JR all over the hospital that night and throughout the next day, which we found out first-hand is a fairly large hospital. Our crew followed to every new wing and every new private waiting room. One of us – Tanner, Anthony, Richie, or myself – was with JR at all times, while our wives were keeping Shelby informed of every new development. We took shifts, but nobody really slept. My son, Tyler, who was twelve at the time, would occasionally ball-up in a chair for a brief nap. But he was more concerned with making sure his buddy Junior was okay. We all agreed to not leave until Shelby could get there. I will forever be proud of everyone in that crew. Around 20 hours later, Shelby finally made it to Houston. We gave them their space and headed back to our house to finally get some sleep.

Over the next few months, while JR was rehabbing at TIRR Memorial in Houston, I got to see one of the best displays of positivity I've ever seen. JR is known as a hard worker. He far surpassed that reputation during rehab. Despite no feeling from the belly button down, JR always pushed harder than he was asked by his physical therapists. He never once complained. Professional rodeo athletes from all over the world made the trip to Houston at some point to visit JR – rodeo truly is one big family. If anyone had anything negative or depressing to say, he immediately shut that down. His hard-working, positive attitude was contagious.

A funny side note to this whole story … our address was the one listed for fans wanting to send their support to JR. During an interview on some news site, he mentioned that Reese's Peanut Butter Cups were his favorite candy. At one point, we had *boxes* of Reese's Peanut Butter Cups sitting in our garage because people kept sending them for him, even though he had already moved on to Utah for his next stage of rehab.

JR's recovery, and his subsequent transition to the reining horse competition world despite the loss of feeling in his legs, has been well documented across social media, television, and popular podcasts. With the hundreds of thousands of people who showed support to JR throughout his recovery journey, he has always had the heart to give back. I'm honored that he and Shelby chose me to be a

Board Member for their Spur Your Way Out Foundation. At the time of this book's writing, the organization is still in its early planning stages. JR and Shelby's "The Spur Your Way Out Show" podcast has already launched, and the non-profit should be launching, or close to launching, around the same time this book is published. The goal of the organization is to raise money to buy track chairs, robotic legs, wheel chair ramps, wheel chair accessible vehicles, etc. for paraplegics in need. I am excited to see all of the people the foundation will help once it does launch. I couldn't be more proud of JR and Shelby.

If my story isn't enough to light a fire under you, then let my brother and JR's stories inspire you. They both continue to inspire me daily today. But back in 2004, when I was facing my own career-ending adversity, bitterness was blinding me to any other possibility than me being a failure in life.

I needed a full life-reset. I eventually packed up all of my belongings and ran. I ran from rodeo. I ran from my friends. I had to get away from the atmosphere that I felt I had let down. The only thing bringing me joy at that time was my new fiancé. So I drove to Las Cruces, New Mexico, where she was going to college, and I moved in with her best friend's boyfriend. As far as I was concerned, I could go the rest of my life without being involved with anything "rodeo" ever again.

We got married. We moved to Texas when I took a job as a worship and youth pastor of a growing church in Montgomery, Texas – Lone Star Cowboy Church. I should have been elated with my life. But I wasn't. Over the next six or seven years, I fought a lot of anger. I was never an angry person before. Most people would tab me as the exact opposite. But now I could snap at the drop of a dime. I didn't know why.

I didn't know anything about my concussion issues and their side effects yet. So I was trying to navigate myself with all these new feelings and emotions. I would pour my whole heart into the hundreds of teenagers I was blessed to lead at Lone Star, but then I would regress into my office, bottling my own issues to hide from everyone around me, including my family.

I struggled with my identity. If I wasn't a bull rider anymore, who was I really? I was trying to cling to my old identity, while watching my relevance to that sport slip deeper into the abyss – something many athletes struggle with after their careers end. Instead of facing my feelings head-on, I tried to "cowboy up" through them. I'm a cowboy. Any sign of weakness is a slight to my toughness.

By this time, a large part of our group of childhood friends had already qualified to numerous NFRs, some of them even winning World Titles. Not only childhood friends from South Dakota, but our friends from

Wyoming, Colorado, and many other places we rodeoed as kids, were now the new stars of the PRCA. I should be happy for them! But it was hard to watch my childhood friends, knowing that I didn't get to fulfill my dream alongside them. It was never a feeling of jealousy towards them. I was *beyond* excited for *them*. I was angry for *me*. I chalked it up internally as being angry with myself; angry that I was a failure. That was the biggest problem: I kept it all bottled up internally.

At the root of all that anger was my bitterness. I was feeling sorry for myself and my situation. That's when my brother wrecked me with one statement. In a conversation on the phone, where he was celebrating the success of one of our closest friends, I said "Ya. But it kind of sucks not getting to be there with him."

My brother replied "*You can get bitter. Or you can get better. But you can't be both.*"

It was like he slapped me upside the head and out of my self-pity trance. Here I am feeling sorry for myself, the whole time not realizing my brother had every right to be more bitter than me. While I had full confidence that I would have qualified to the NFR, PBR World Finals, or both, there was no question that Nate would have qualified to the NFR *multiple* times, had he not been injured. Yet he chose to take the higher road and not focus on things out of his hands.

That moment changed me. If it hadn't, I would hate to think of where I would be today. I thought the career-ending injury would be the hardest adversity I would have to face in life. The future would prove it was far from the hardest. If I hadn't learned to defeat bitterness at this point in my life, still in my early 20's, I would have never been able to face the even harder challenges that laid ahead.

Chapter 9

The Concussion That Broke the Camel's Brain

Nick (25) working on his newly purchased dirt-track race car with his son Tyler (2) in 2007; three years after his career-ending injury. Photo courtesy of Ivy Morrison

When I was told I couldn't ride bulls anymore, what's the next most logical thing I should do to fill my need for adrenaline? If your answer is "buy a dirt-track race car," then you are correct.

I have always been a fan of racing. The reality is I'm just a fan of competition, period. I could sit intently and watch two old women knit, as long as they are racing each other. I know I am not the only one who, as a kid sitting in the backseat of the car on a rainy day, would watch the water droplets form on the window and then race each other down to the bottom, announcing the race between the droplets in my head.

It was the fall of 2007, a little over three years after my last bull riding injury. I was 25 years old at this point. I had been going to a local dirt track with a friend to help him with his sprint car. The opportunity arose for me to purchase an asphalt-track hobby stock car and convert it to a dirt-track car to race on my own. I didn't even hesitate. If I could dominate my friends in go-karts, how much harder could this be? Turns out, it's quite a bit harder. It was more like go-karts on steroids driving across ice. And wow, was it fun. I was very inexperienced compared to most of the other drivers, but I had a blast doing it.

It took a few months of racing until I was finally starting to get it figured out enough that I could run at a fairly good pace. I wasn't racing for the win yet, but at least I could see the leaders in front of me. Before that, the only time I would see the leaders was as they were lapping me. I had my own group of drivers around the same experience level as me, and we would have our own races against each other while the more experienced drivers were racing for the win.

One night, it was particularly dry. When the track gets dry, big clouds of dust are created, entering the corners, where the tires are sliding against the dirt at their fastest speeds. This can hinder your vision quite a bit going into those corners. It's already hard enough to see beyond the car in front of you on a clear day. If you add in all of that dust, you can now barely see anything. Driving on dirt is all about the feel of the car and adapting to the sounds around you. You aren't allowed to have mirrors or a spotter radioing to your helmet. So, you have to judge where other cars are by the volume of their engines. What seems like chaos is happening in a hurry, and you have to make split-second decisions to adapt to everything going on around you.

On this night, I was running in about 10th place out of 24 drivers in the main event. It was one lap after a restart so all of the cars were bunched together. I was in the outside lane with cars directly in front, behind, and on my left. At the far end of the front straightaway right before entering turn one, which is usually the fastest part of the track, the driver in front of me "checked up" hard on his brakes to avoid hitting another car sliding up into his lane. I checked up as well to keep from running into the back of him. The driver behind me didn't see any of this happening and kept plowing into the corner, slamming into the back of my car, and spinning me down to the bottom. Usually, drivers would see this happening in front of them and slow down in an attempt to save their own car. Due to the thick cloud of dust, nobody saw the wreck until the last second. The first cars directly behind scrambled to miss me, but this left the drivers directly behind them helpless. By the time they saw the wreck, it was too late. When my car started to spin towards the bottom, another car hit the nose of mine, spinning my front end back to the right and into the nose of another car passing the wreck on that side. That swung me back around to the left again. I came to rest with the nose of my car facing the infield, sitting perpendicular to the track.

My car was mangled but I seemed unharmed inside the protective roll cage welded to the interior. I thought the wreck was finished and started to relax when, all of a sudden, another driver came screaming into the corner. He didn't see any of the wreck due to the large cloud of dust. I saw the nose of his car come out of the cloud just as he hit, full speed, into my driver's door.

My next memory was a track safety-crew worker snapping his fingers in front of the face of my helmet. I tried to play off the fact that I was just knocked out and convince the safety worker I was fine. I was pretty experienced in the getting-knocked-out department, and didn't want to make a big deal about it. This, literally, was not my first rodeo. I stayed in the car as it was hooked to a tow truck, pulled off of the track, and into the pits. I wasn't that worried about being knocked out again. I was more disappointed in the fact that my car I had just bought less than a year ago was now totaled. I had been through being knocked out so many times I didn't think it was going to be any issue whatsoever.

I truly don't know what was different about this concussion. It's almost like my brain was on the edge of a cliff from so many other concussions, and this was the one that pushed it over. On its surface, this seemed like any other concussion. I had the normal hazy cloud around my vision and thoughts, although this time that "cloud" wasn't going away after a few days like it did after past concussions. I felt somewhat nauseous, but nothing unusual considering the circumstances. My body was sore from the crash, but other than the continuing cloudy vision, nothing else seemed out of the ordinary to me. To my wife, however, a lot changed.

My wife knows me better than anyone. She knows all of my moods and nuances. Almost immediately, she started to see signs of a completely different husband. I went from being one of the most patient people she knew, to getting mad when the faucet water wouldn't heat up fast enough for my liking. I became extremely irritable and hard to be around. Every little thing seemed to set me off. The worst part is, I never even noticed. The people closest to me noticed a change, but I didn't comprehend any abnormalities in my behavior whatsoever.

There were little things that, looking back, I can see were progressively becoming an issue. But after that night, they accelerated into me becoming a type of person I grew to hate. My biggest regret in life is the person I became over that next two-to-three-year period, before I could figure out what was going on and learn how to get a handle on it. Whenever anything would happen, I would immediately think the worst possible scenario would follow. I was paranoid that every person around me was against me or trying to ruin my reputation.

My motto in life had always been, *"If I take care of my character, my reputation will take care of itself"*. But now my only concern became my reputation, not my character. By putting my focus on trying to "impress" with my reputation, I instead greatly damaged my character. That's something you can never get back with some people. The reality was I didn't need to try to impress people. I was extremely successful in my current work. I had a life, leading up to this point, that most people would be jealous of. Yet there was an emptiness there; a part of me that knew I didn't quite fulfill my entire destiny. I knew what I *should* have accomplished in life, yet I felt like I never fully got that opportunity. I was convinced in my mind that people wouldn't like me for who I was as a person, but only if they viewed me as successful.

Growing up looking like Steve Erkle's white cousin made my main source of approval come through my bull riding success. I was unpopular during the week at school, but extremely popular amongst my rodeo friends on weekends. This made me think that the only time people truly liked me was when I was riding bulls successfully. This is an extremely unstable philosophy to live under because, as anyone in rodeo can attest, it quickly becomes a sport of "what have you done for me lately?"

Much like many sports, your stature among your peers is highly predicated on your *recent* successes. Unless you walk away from your rodeo career with a World Title, or some great achievement that stands out in their mind, most people forget you even existed in the sport. It's one of the very few things I don't like about rodeo. When you are winning, everyone is your friend. When you are struggling over a long period of time, your popularity dwindles immensely. When your career is over, you find out who your true friends are. You learn to weed out the people who were only your friend as long as your friendship added something of value to them.

Numerous rodeo athletes face this type of feeling of abandonment, on many levels, when their career is over. This isn't because rodeo people are "bad people." They are *great* people; some of the best I have ever been around!

This is more a result of rodeo having such a high turnover rate than it is anything nefarious. There are numerous talented rodeo athletes who could be stars in the sport. Only a small percentage of those can handle the stress of the "rodeo road" that includes hundreds of thousands of miles worth of driving, a strict workout regime, high expenses, numerous injuries, surgeries, rehab from surgeries, and long dry spells in-between paychecks. An even smaller percentage can stay healthy long enough to have a full career. When that career is over, the next wave of talent is already replacing them. When you are around each other almost daily, it is easier to think of that person. When their career is over, you don't see each other as often, so they aren't in the forefront of your mind. This leads to a feeling of abandonment by those who are no longer rodeoing full time.

This isn't just a "rodeo" problem, though. This phenomenon seems to happen in anything that involves recognizing success. Outside of the superstars, we only remember who is in the spotlight at the moment. I challenge you to try and remember every player from the World Series-winning baseball team from five years ago. Other than the most dedicated of fans, most people may only remember the players who were a major factor in that series and nobody else. This is human nature. You can see why, though, it was so volatile to think my only approval was in my bull riding success. I have since changed this mindset, but at the time, it only compounded my issues.

Many athletes struggle with finding their identity once they no longer have the sport they, and so many others, identified them for. It's a hard transition to make from life in the spotlight to life without it. Over the years, I have been blessed to kindle friendships with many professional athletes from numerous sports. This is a conversation I have had with many of them.

"Finding your new identity" is something I have watched many friends struggle with when it comes time for them to leave the sport they have always been a part of. I think it's even worse when your career ends early and abruptly due to injuries. There is a feeling of a lack of accomplishment that can slowly eat away at your innermost soul. Your mind is constantly flooded with the "what if"s. To this day I struggle watching a PBR on television. It drowns me in a small depression anytime I watch, as it becomes a reminder of how close to living my dream I truly got.

When your career is over, and you are back in the real world, you have to face the reality of "what do I do now?" When, throughout your entire life, people introduced you with your name followed immediately by your occupation, it's easy to see how that is conceived as your only identity. I went from "This is my friend Nick

Morrison. He's a professional bull rider" to "This is my friend Nick Morrison. He's a.....umm....what is it you do now?" Those first few years, you might as well have said, "This is my friend Nick Morrison. He's a grade-A bonafide *loser*!!"

When concussions are already giving you dark thoughts, the difficulty of a transition like this doesn't help any. You feel like you have to live up to the hype of your former life. Then, when people don't know you from your former life, you feel like you have to hype that perception up to them yourself. Some people deal with this better than others. Not me. I struggled immensely with it. In full transparency, early after my career was over, this was a battle I lost almost every day.

"Acceptance" is something that *many* people struggle with. The sheer value we put on acceptance causes us to do things we wouldn't normally do. This goes back to our behavior as kids all the way through adulthood.

It took one of the worst days of my life, which you will read about later, for me to finally get a handle on this. I learned that I couldn't *afford* to go through life trying to please everyone else. Even then, it didn't just "happen". I had to change my entire way of thinking to overcome this. I had to realize my long-term value could no longer be placed in what people think of me; it has to be placed in what *God* thinks of me. People are always going to disappoint. Why? Because we are human. When I put my faith in people, and my value in what people thought of me, I was becoming a person living nowhere near the standards I wanted to hold myself to. Then, when I felt I was close to finally attaining their approval, I found out it was always a moving target. What I didn't realize, by the sheer act of trying to gain people's approval I, in turn, started losing their respect.

My new attitude on life is that I would rather people think less of me and be surprised, than think more of me and be disappointed.

Ultimately, I want to be the best man I can possibly be, and strive to be the man God designed me to be. Do I have it completely under control? No. Will I someday? I sure hope so. Is it better? 100 times.

This is a continual work in progress. Two common hidden side-effects of multiple concussions is constant paranoia towards others, as well as paranoia towards yourself of never feeling like you are "enough." I have to force myself to fight against those urges, and be confident in the man I am today; not the man I *could have been* if things had happened differently. I've had to learn to change my focus when becoming inundated with the "what if"s. Stop focusing on the past, and start focusing on the future.

It's easy to say, *"Well these are my side effects now so I'm just going to have to deal with it."* That's the easy road. If I took the easy road, due to my concussions, I more than likely would have run off every single person close to me.

The motto in our house for the past six-plus years has been "no excuses." I can only control what I can control moving forward. The past is the past. Other people's opinions should have no effect on my work ethic. What they think should have no effect on my self-worth. If I can't do "that" anymore, what *can* I do? Those old dreams may be shattered, but I still have a lot of life ahead of me. So, stop wasting it focusing on "what could have been," and start paving myself a new dream.

It would be years before I had many of these realizations. I first endured years of struggling, learning myself, and learning to handle life *despite* the new difficulties and behavioral changes brought on by all of my concussions.

As time passed, it would materialize that those behavioral changes were not the worst complication to arise from the "racing concussion." They were just the tip of the iceberg. Within a few weeks, I started noticing blood trickling from my nose on occasion. Usually I would have written this off as "dry air," but I was living close to Houston, Texas. The only time "dry" is used in a Houstonian's vocabulary is when they are talking about the dry rub on the brisket they are about to smoke. It's so hot and humid here that you break into a sweat simply by opening your front door. No, my nosebleeds were definitely not from dry air.

So that left me deducing these nosebleeds couldn't mean anything good. I've seen all those virus movies. When someone has blood trickling from their nose, it usually means they are going to die. Either that, or become a zombie. But even then I didn't want to go to a doctor. If I was going to die, I was going to die. No need dying and leaving my wife with a huge doctor bill just so a doctor could tell me, "Yep, your nose is definitely bleeding." So like a true cowboy, I ignored it.

Shortly afterwards, I started passing out. The first time it happened, I didn't know what to think. I was jogging up the stairs in our youth building, skipping two steps at a time like I always did. The next thing I knew my body hurt and I was balled-up in a corner at the bottom. Apparently I passed out and rolled down a whole flight of stairs. Shaking it off in confusion, I got up, started to run up the stairs again, and once again woke up laying at the bottom. Once I recovered, sensing a pattern I *walked* up the stairs. I didn't know it at the time, but we would find out later that a spike in heart-rate – which my brain interprets delayed before sending blood in one big rush to my head to catch-up – is often a contributing factor to me passing out.

After that day, passing out was progressively happening more often. In my logic, as long as my wife didn't know about the nosebleeds or me passing out, then she wouldn't make me go to a doctor. And as long as it didn't happen in front of somebody else, I was able to hide it from everyone in my life. I don't know how long I would have gone without seeing a doctor if it hadn't been for the "Madden Incident" happening right there in front of my wife and friend.

My friend Nate Dove, who we call Indy, and I were at my house playing Madden on my Xbox. I had a win streak going against Indy that was in jeopardy, as I was down by 12 points with only fifteen seconds left in the game. All of you Madden players know the pride, and smack talk, that was on the line here. I couldn't let him win without at least trying to keep my streak alive. So I threw a Hail Mary pass. He jokingly dove his players to the ground, attempting to rub in the fact that he didn't believe I stood a chance of winning that game. I scored an easy touchdown with four seconds left but was still down by 5 points. I called for an onside kick, which even *if* I recovered it, my virtual player would be tackled immediately. There was no doubt in my mind that he had won this game, which he was reminding me of as he stood in front of me taunting.

Then the craziest thing happened. My player picked up the onside kick and nobody tackled him. Indy was running his players away from the ball in a strategy to burn the last four seconds off the clock without touching my player down. He was trying to prevent me still having time left over for another Hail Mary. He over-played his hand. I controlled my player to take off running. After breaking through the only tackler left, my player had wide-open green grass in front of him. 40-yard line. 50-yard line. 40. 30. Indy is screaming "no no no no no" at the top of his lungs. 20. 10. 5. Touchdown. I win! I stood up fast, half screaming, half laughing, and WAM!!

I woke up a good fifteen feet from where I was previously standing, balled up in the corner of the doorway, to the sight of Indy and my wife standing over me looking bewildered. Evidently, when I passed out, my body tried to catch itself and it looked like I had lost my balance falling backwards. They told me I ran backwards as I slammed hard into the wall on my way down.

The gig was up. I now had to tell my wife that I have been having issues with passing out. And just like I suspected would happen, she wanted me to see a doctor, just to make sure everything was ok. Looking back, I am glad I did.

When I first went to the doctor, he tried to find conventional reasons as to why I was passing out. He sent me for tests that had to deal with blood pressure, tumors, heart issues, cancer, pretty much anything he could think of. My arm looked like a plucked porcupine with all the different blood tests they drew. After these tests revealed nothing out of the ordinary, other than some internal injuries and shifting of organs due to hitting the ground too hard too many times, the doctors were just as confused as I was.

I was starting to experience an increasing number of memory lapses, cognitive troubles, and motor skill difficulties. I don't know why I never thought to tie those issues to the passing out issues as well. But when I finally told the doctor about those, he shifted the focus to my brain. That's when everything finally started making sense, and my view on life would be forever changed.

Chapter 10

My Lightbulb Epiphany

Nick (17) speaking at the Cowboy Church Service before the South Dakota High School Regional Finals Rodeo in Sturgis, SD in 2000. Photo Courtesy of Mary Scott

WHEN WE FIRST BEGAN CONNECTING MY CONCUSSIONS TO the health issues I was facing, in 2008-2009, the public study of long-term effects of multiple concussions on a single person was still in its infancy. It definitely wasn't an issue the average person outside of the medical world talked about. It wouldn't be until a few years later, May 2, 2012, that the entire sports world took a closer look at concussions. It was a few more years after that, January 9, 2017, that the danger of multiple concussions hit too close to home for the rodeo world as well. Sadly, in both instances, it took someone taking their own life for the seriousness of the issue to be taken as earnestly as it is today.

Retired San Diego Chargers star linebacker Junior Seau was found dead in his home on May 2, 2012, from a self-inflicted gunshot wound to the chest[1]. As a lifelong, die-hard Denver Broncos fan, I grew up keeping an eye on the Chargers since they were one of the rivals of my favorite team. I always respected, and even admired, Seau's talent and demeanor. I followed his career closely, despite him being on a rival team. Some fans believe you have to hate every team and player from a division rivalry. That's not me. I respect talent and hard work. If a player leaves it all on the field, I typically like to watch

1. Farmer, Sam. "Junior Seau Had Brain Disease When He Committed Suicide." *Los Angeles Times*, Los Angeles Times, 10 Jan. 2013, www.latimes.com/sports/la-xpm-2013-jan-10-la-sp-sn-junior-seau-brain-20130110-story.html.

them play, regardless of what team they play for. To get to that level of competition takes hard work that most people don't see. To become an *elite* player at that level is even more impressive. So, Seau was always at the top of my list of players I admired.

When the news broke about his death, I followed the story closely. As the days passed and more information came out about it, I took even more interest when the experts started linking his suicide to his past concussions. This was the first time I had ever heard of concussions being linked to suicidal thoughts. While watching medical experts elaborate more on a sports-talk show one evening, they started talking about something else I had never heard of before that day: CTE.

CTE stands for Chronic Traumatic Encephalopathy. According to the Boston University CTE Center, "CTE is a degenerative brain disease found in people with repetitive brain trauma where a protein called Tau forms clumps that slowly spread throughout the brain killing brain cells."[2]

In simpler terms, CTE causes atrophy, or wasting away, of brain cells that spreads, disrupting normal brain func-

---

2. McKee, Ann C., and Robert C. Cantu, et al. "Chronic Traumatic Encephalopathy in Athletes: Progressive Tauopathy After Repetitive Head Injury." *Boston University CTE Research Center*, American Association of Neuropathologists, Inc., 1 July 2009, www.researchgate.net/publication/259342091_Kumar_etal_JNEN.

and deteriorating the brain over time. In the simplest of terms, it is gradually eating holes throughout the brain.

The Boston University CTE Center goes on to say, "Early symptoms are not said to start appearing until a patient's late 20s and early 30s. These symptoms have an effect on the person's mood or behavior, which include depression, irritability, aggression, impulse control problems, and paranoia. More exposed blows to the head can start causing patients to see cognitive symptoms that include impaired judgment, memory loss, and confusion."[3]

As I sat there watching these medical experts describe CTE, and all of the symptoms Junior Seau had faced, I felt like that meme of Leonardo DiCaprio sitting in the recliner pointing at the TV going, "That's me! ... That's also me!". Every single thing these experts were saying was describing my struggles exactly.

At my next appointment with my neurologist, I asked if he could test me for CTE. He informed me that CTE can only be diagnosed *post*-death because it requires taking slices of the brain as samples. He said he hadn't brought it up yet because there was no way to test for it on a live patient, but CTE had always been on his mind with my situation, from the first day I was sent to his office. Even though he couldn't medically diagnose CTE,

---

3. McKee

he also told me that his off-the-record opinion was that he was convinced I had a severe case of it.

That was 2012. CTE wasn't as prevalent in public conversations about concussions as it is today. While the only way to officially confirm CTE currently is post-death, technology is always advancing. At the time of writing this book, there are reportedly great advances being made in CTE diagnosis. The goal is to eventually develop a way to scan for Tau protein clumps in the brain while the patient is still alive.

The incident that got the attention of the rodeo world was the death of professional bull rider Ty Pozzobon in 2017.[4] I didn't know Ty personally, but I have a lot of friends who did. When I've talked to people who knew him, everyone has had nothing but great things to say about the kid. Ty was considered the best bull rider from Canada at the time, before tragically taking his own life at only 25 years of age. To my knowledge, Ty was the first confirmed case of CTE in a rodeo athlete.

What I witnessed over the next few months, after the news of his death came out, was amazing. Facebook was flooded with one story after another from professional rodeo athletes and their spouses, sharing what they are

---

4. Klinkenberg, Marty. "How Ty Pozzobon's Suicide Forced Bull Riding to Confront Its Quiet Concussion Crisis." *The Globe and Mail*, The Globe and Mail, 7 Nov. 2017, www.theglobeandmail.-com/sports/ty-pozzobon-concussion-bull-riding/article36842612/.

dealing with personally as a result of repeated concussions. By this time, I had already made my concussion struggles public. But I only knew of a few other rodeo friends who were struggling as well, and only because of private conversations we had. Very few people were willing to publicly acknowledge it for fear of being branded a derogatory term for "wimp." After Ty's death, something rodeo athletes never wanted to talk about publicly was now at the forefront of every conversation. I had one conversation with a World Champion calf roper who told me he is convinced that every professional rodeo athlete, no matter what discipline they compete in, has had at least one concussion. We are constantly around animals with kicking feet and slinging heads. It's bound to happen.

Ty's death was tragic. It shook the rodeo world to its core. But instead of sweeping the root of the issue – repeated concussions – under the rug after his death, the rodeo world finally embraced efforts to fix the problem. Ty's family has been *monumental* in this movement through the Ty Pozzobon Foundation.

Looking back, I don't blame anyone but myself for the issues I deal with today. I made the choice *every* time to get back on. Me. Nobody else *made* me. Could the PBR and PRCA have had more protocols in place to prevent the epidemic of snowballing concussions back then? If the conclusion is only made in a vacuum, then the answer is "yes". But it's not that simple. In reality, *nobody* was looking at concussions seriously back then. They didn't have the research and scientific studies that we have today.

To look back at sports injuries with what we know today and say "sports organizations should have done better" is like looking back at David from the Bible and criticizing him for not being able to shred Eddy Van Halen's "Eruption" on his lyre. We didn't have the *knowledge* then that we have now. We didn't have the *technology* then that we have now. Instead of looking back and pointing fingers, we need to divert our focus to the future! Every professional or amateur sports organization has to ask themselves, "What can we do moving forward with the knowledge we have today?" While I'm willing to give a pass to how sports handled concussions with limited knowledge in the past, I'm not willing to show that same grace in the future based on what we know now.

I've seen a massive step forward once people began acknowledging head injuries instead of trying to sweep them under the rug. The level of support towards concussion issues today would have been unheard of in the past. I think the biggest advancement we have made in recent years is making it okay to talk about head injuries and removing the stigma that doing so is a sign of weakness. Instead of saying, "It was just a bump on the head, toughen up, and shake it off", we now hear, "His knees are wobbling; we may wanna check on him". That's huge!

Jumping back to when I was first learning of the severities of my concussion issues in 2008-2009, there wasn't the kind of support system in place that there is now. Truthfully, I think my biggest lack of support back then was my unwillingness to *seek* support. If I wasn't willing to tell my wife everything I was dealing with, you better believe I wasn't about to tell anyone else either! I had the cowboy mentality of "*I got myself into this mess, I can get myself out of it.*" If anyone around me witnessed something happen, I just made it seem like some crazy one-off incident and brushed it off. I didn't even let my own *parents* know. I kept fighting my own fight, thinking it would eventually go away.

I didn't want my wife thinking of me as weak, so I was only willing to share my struggles when something happened that exposed those struggles. After the "Madden incident" I was finally willing to tell my wife I was having issues with nosebleeds and passing out. After the complications with my cognitive and motor skills started happening more frequently, I was finally willing to tell my wife I was struggling with the fallout of numerous concussions. Those were all on the surface, and things she could witness with her eyes. She *wanted* to help me, but I would only let her know about what I thought she could already see. What I wasn't willing to tell her was the internal fights I was having; the fights in my mind.

I think it's important to note here that I wasn't fighting depression in any fashion. I was far from depressed. I was

25 years old and married with two outstanding kids. I was pastoring a youth ministry that had grown from our original dozen students to now reaching hundreds of teenagers every week. I was loving life! No, I wasn't depressed. I *was* angry, bitter, and filled with regrets, though. I hadn't learned about CTE yet. I didn't know how dangerously concussions can alter your train of thought. I was just a 25-year-old kid, finally seeing a doctor, and trying to figure out why I was passing out and struggling with simple tasks that never used to be an issue.

Once the doctor pieced together how many concussions I truly had up to that point – this was five years before Junior Seau's death when I learned about CTE – he sent me to a neurologist, which started a year and a half of perpetual testing. I became somewhat of a test-dummy guinea pig. If there was a test or scan for the brain, I probably did it. It's not every day that someone with as many concussions as I had, and still functioning despite them, walks into a neurologist's door. Three to four times a week I was going somewhere around the Houston area for a test.

I did brain function tests, cognitive tests, IQ tests, hand-eye coordination tests, sleep tests, and tests meant to frustrate me just so they could read the reactions my brain was triggering. These tests were very revealing.

One test facility I went to on a weekly basis would time me doing progressively harder puzzles, mind benders, or tasks that made me problem solve through memory, the use of my hands, or both. They found, with my high IQ, I could solve these puzzles at some of the fastest times they had ever recorded. My competitive nature may have had a little something to do with skewing those results too. But every time I would hit a small moment of hesitation, I would completely shut down and not be able to complete even the easiest of tasks anymore. I would also get more visibly frustrated with each time my brain would "lock up." They tried to do these tests in reverse order with the hardest first then progressively getting easier. It had the *same result.* This proved that my brain "locking up" was not due to the difficulty of the task but had to do with brain function itself. Whenever I would "hit a wall," no matter how difficult or easy the task, my brain would completely shut down and now struggle doing the simplest things.

As frustrating as this was, it was also extremely helpful because they taught me to take breaks, something I never wanted to do, when I got tired or started feeling frustration kick in. It also helped me to recognize that I don't want to let my brain win in these situations. I don't ever want to take the easy way out. If I can't remember something, and feel my brain "shutting down" trying to think of it, I will stop thinking, take a deep breath or small break, then make myself remember what I was trying to think of or finish the task at hand. I won't let someone else finish the sentence for me or finish tasks if my hands kept fumbling. That's the easy route. It's my *will* over my *mind* in this situation. It doesn't matter if it takes me all day to accomplish it, or if I break 15 dishes trying. I will eventually finish that task. This is one of the areas where my wife has shown the most patience with me.

In the midst of these tests, I was prescribed at least seven hours a week of playing video games, or around one hour a day, to stimulate my hand-eye coordination and brain reactions. I had no complaints about that prescription as I've always considered myself to be in that first generation of true "gamers." My wife, on the other hand, joked that she wanted a second opinion. Upon hearing this, our neurologist consulted a second doctor walking by his office who thought I should actually be playing at least *14* hours a week. I liked the route this was heading and asked Ivy if she wanted a third opinion. She relented to the 14-hours-a-week diagnostic.

One game he wanted me to play was a brand-new game that had just come out that year: Minecraft. Like he told me, "Why should I have you coming in and playing with blocks at a table when you can be building with unlimited blocks at home?" So I would take time every night to play Minecraft with my son, Tyler, who was around four years old when I got this diagnosis. This game was great at forcing my brain to deduce the process of building structures from the ground up. Plus, it was a fun bonding time with my son. I don't do things small. If I'm going to do something, I'm putting my whole heart into it and we are going all out.

Over the next fifteen years, my son and I built cities together, amusement parks, and massive mansions of every design on Minecraft. We even built a life-sized replica Denver Broncos Mile High Stadium – complete with locker rooms, bathrooms, concessions, and individual suites. Some of these projects took us over a year each to complete. When my daughter, Gracie, was old enough, she even joined in the fun of the family Minecraft therapy. It's the first time I ever enjoyed saying, "It looks like it is time for me to take my prescription."

In all honesty, I rarely come close to playing 14 hours a week, because, as busy as I am, I rarely have 14 hours a week to spare. But my wife has become the biggest believer in this "prescription." There are days where she will actually force me to take the entire day off to do nothing *but* play video games. Surprisingly we have both noticed a huge difference in everything from my cognitive skills, to dexterity, to even my mood or behavior after the times I have played. As crazy as this type of prescription sounds, it also makes comprehensive sense. It forces my brain to solve problems, think quickly, evaluate situations, and make decisions while using hand-eye coordination at the same time.

As my issues have progressively become worse over time, I can no longer play fast-paced multiplayer video games. They actually cause an *adverse* reaction now. It is too strenuous on my brain to process all of the moving parts happening at the same time. Plus, my reflexes are so delayed in reacting to an online shooter on Call of Duty, it doesn't really help with my short-fuse struggles. Or, as it's been presented to me in medical terms: "impulse control problems."

I had so many different types of tests run during this period of time, it is actually hard to remember what all was tested. One of the earliest tests was the most revealing though. They hooked sensors all over my head, laid me on my back, then slid me into a tube similar to a CT scan machine. There was a monitor inside directly above my face. On that screen would scroll various things like a picture, words, math problems, etc. They asked me to either say out loud what I was seeing, or solve the problem that showed on the screen. If it was a picture of a bird, for instance, I would simply say "bird." Some pictures were easy to decipher what they were, while others were more like ink blots that are left up to the interpretation of the person looking at them. If it was words on the screen I would simply read them out loud. Once again some were easy words and some made you really think on how to pronounce them. Math problems I had to solve, so on and so forth. Periodically they would come over a speaker and give me a problem to solve audibly, or ask me to raise my right arm, wiggle a toe, etc. These different variances would trigger different sections of my brain. The sensors on my head would pick up what portion of the brain was being used and it would light up little dots around that area on a monitor the doctors were watching.

They gave us a DVD recording of the test afterwards, or else I wouldn't have believed what the tests showed. With each task, different sensors, targeted at specific lobes of the brain, would light up, corresponding with the functions of that lobe. When something came up on the screen that was supposed to trigger the right frontal lobe, that area of my brain wasn't lighting up on the monitor at all. Instead, the *rest* of the brain had little dots scattered throughout the other sensors.

The brain is an amazing organ. It reacts and adapts to its surroundings. Since I was considered a very strong right-brained person, and since the concussions happened over time, the rest of my brain apparently adapted and "picked up the slack," so to speak, when the front-right lobe of my brain started shutting down due to too many blows to that specific area. They found signs of slight damage to different areas of the brain as well, but most of it was to the frontal lobes. We really don't know if the higher IQ aided in this phenomenon or not. That hypothesis has been thrown around, though, as an explanation for why my brain continued functioning at a high rate, despite the tests showing I should have lost far more motor and speaking skills than I had.

Where most people would be devastated with the news I received after each test result, I became encouraged. I now knew what was wrong and could focus my attention and approach. I finally had a direction. I hate the feeling of not knowing what's going on. I want to be in control, know every detail, and be equipped to influence my own destiny. The determination to improve has always been there. "Settle" is not a word in the Morrison family's vocabulary. A phrase that is? "*Good enough, isn't.*" Every mistake or every success is just another opportunity to improve.

That's not just a mentality of our family. That's a mentality of proven winners. Years earlier, during a PBR event in Bismarck, North Dakota, Adriano Moraes and I stayed up all night in our hotel room talking. He had already won two of his three PBR World Titles at this point, and since he was in a talkative mood that night, I was a sponge trying to soak in as much knowledge as I could. Not every 19-year-old gets to have the kind of heart-to-heart conversation with one of the greatest to ever compete in their sport, like I did that night.

We talked about everything from God, our childhoods, our futures, and riding bulls. Diving into his mind, I realized how brilliant he truly is, and the geometrical genius that fueled the success of his bull riding career. He said something during the conversation that has stuck in my mind ever since. "You should always be improving. The moment you think you're the best, and settle for being the best, is the moment you're no longer the best. Everyone working to improve will pass you, and leave you where you settled." At that time I took the advice as meaning towards my bull riding, as I imagined my future would be full of many years worth of riding bulls with many accomplishments along the way. I didn't expect to have my career end two years later. That advice, however, has fueled every other aspect of my life since.

The diagnosis I received for my brain could not become an excuse. If I let it be an excuse, that meant I would be settling for my circumstances. With direction, I now knew what I could focus on and what areas I could improve in. If your mind accepts defeat, your body soon follows. For the first time in years, I finally had a new beast to conquer.

Chapter 11

The Quarter Incident

Nick (28) speaking at Crossfire Youth Ministries of Lone Star Cowboy Church in 2010 Photo courtesy of Kevyn Schneider Photography

I don't know if it was the cowboy mentality, the rancher mentality, the rodeo mentality, the manly mentality, a combination of all of the above, or plain and simple pride that prevented me from wanting people to know about my struggles from my injuries. I felt like it was a weakness that others wouldn't understand. I tried to find ways to "blow off" what just happened and hope nobody would inquire deeper into it. I became very good at covering up my issues from those around me and hiding what was actually happening.

My wife knew how much it embarrassed me to pass out in front of people, or to have a brain episode and not recognize anyone in the room. This is one of the many areas in which she has proven to be a phenomenal spouse. The reality is I wouldn't be able to deal with half of this stuff if she wasn't so amazing. We are talking about a woman who went back to college and double-majored – graduating summa cum laude with a 4.0 GPA in *both* Bachelor's Degrees, I might add – so she could take classes on brain injuries for the sole reason of understanding me better, and knowing how to help me. She also knew I wanted as few people as possible to know about what I perceived as a weakness. So she would do whatever she could to protect me in the moment.

One instance really stands out in my mind. We had a bunch of guests over to our house for a get-together around Christmas time. I went to flip the power strip on for our tree lights. It was behind the tree and near the back of one of our living room chairs. As I leaned over the chair to reach the switch, I passed out, sprawled across the arm of the chair. She saw it happen and recognized immediately what was going on. She walked over and sat on the corner of the chair next to me, blocking me from the view of others. She put her hand on my back and talked to me as if I was still conscious but having troubles getting the lights on. Within a few minutes, I woke up. She gave me a look to make sure I was ok, then another look that said, "You better stay in this chair until you get all your chickens back into the henhouse", and then went back to her normal conversation like nothing had happened. To this day, I don't think anyone there even knows I was passed out at all.

We did let a few certain people know the small essential details about my issues. For instance, my boss at the new church I was working at, Dayton Christian Center in Dayton, Texas, and his wife knew. We also had a few friends who knew, just so I had others present who understood what was going on in case something went wrong when I was around them and my wife wasn't close. But even then, it was a very small, trusted circle of friends. Some of my closest rodeo friends also knew because they were dealing with the same things. You can't underestimate the importance of having those friends, just so you have someone to talk about it with. They understand what you are going through in a way nobody else can, because they live it as well.

One of those friends who has become a rock for me is Heath Ford. I've known Heath most of my life. As we competed against each other growing up, Heath and the entire Ford clan from Colorado became instant friends with us Morrison boys from South Dakota. Heath's professional rodeo career, as a bareback rider and bull rider, lasted over 20 years and included multiple trips to the NFR in the bareback riding. He's one of the few people I know who has probably had as many concussions as I've had. We have numerous conversations about what we deal with and how we have learned to adjust or cope. It's common for one of us to text the other when something new happens with "Have you ever had this happen to you?"

Our wives also talk to each other about our issues – another thing I highly recommend if you are dealing with post-concussion effects. It's good for your spouse to have another spouse to talk to. The mood swings, short tempers, memory issues, and other symptoms can be as stressful for your spouse as they are for you. If spouses can connect and converse with each other, it may help them both understand their own spouses better. Talking to others can help them understand that their spouse's anger is not geared towards them at that moment; it's just the frustration going on in their head that they can't find a way to communicate.

Heath is great at protecting me as well. Just like with my wife, he can "cover up" my passing-out with the best of them. One of many incidents when this happened took place in Houston, Texas, during Rodeo Houston, one of the highest-paying rodeos of the year. Since it was close to where I was living, I drove down to hang out in the locker room with friends who were in town competing at the rodeo. I was helping Heath, who was riding in the bareback riding that night, and the other friends with pulling their ropes, riggins, and saddles. After the performance we rode in the contestant shuttle van from the Houston Texans' NRG Stadium, where the rodeo is held, to the contestant area off-site where my car was parked, and where Ted and Linda Weise held nightly bible studies for the contestants and their families. Every big rodeo has an area like this, complete with stalls for the contestants' horses, hook-ups for their campers/trailers/rodeo rigs, and a big hospitality tent serving complimentary breakfast and lunch every day. The contestant area for Rodeo Houston is about a five-mile drive from NRG Stadium.

If I am riding in a vehicle, especially a van, and the driver makes a sharp enough turn without my eyes looking at the road, I will pass out without any warning. I can only guess this happens because my eyes aren't seeing the cause of the sudden movement, and my brain can't process why I'm turning suddenly. I never have this issue if I am driving or intently watching the road as a passenger. When this particular incident happened, it was one of the first times I had passed out in this manner, and something I hadn't yet learned to anticipate. I was sitting in the back of the van next to Heath and his wife, Britt. Sure enough, the driver took a sharp turn, probably dodging the traffic of 60,000+ fans leaving the facility, and I passed out right into Heath's shoulder. According to Britt, Heath just put his arm around me and acted like we were having a private conversation until I woke up.

Things like that can happen with Heath and we laugh about it later. He's that kind of friend. It's not new either. I remember one year in Las Vegas, during the Wrangler National Finals Rodeo, he and I were down on the arena floor helping out in front of the chutes during the Permit Holder of the Year Challenge. This is an event my brother produces as a part of the Benny Binion's World Famous NFR Bucking Horse and Bull Sale at the South Point Casino and Resort. It's put on by the PRCA, and features the next crop of young up-and-coming professional talent already competing in the PRCA on their permit. Think of it like an MLB All-Star Futures Game. Numerous eventual World Champions and NFR Qualifiers have been featured at this event throughout the years. It kicks off the entire 10-Day NFR festivities on Thursday morning, with the First Round of the NFR happening at the Thomas and Mack Center later that evening.

During the bull riding portion of the rodeo, a bull that had just bucked off his rider came running around to where we were standing. We climbed up the front of the chute we were in front of to avoid getting hit. This was nothing out of the ordinary and happens quite often at rodeos. But in the process of reaching up, grabbing the top rail, and pulling myself up, my shoulder dislocated out of socket. Heath, directly next to me, heard that distinct sound of bone grinding and popping that happens with a dislocation. He looked over at me and said, "She's out again, isn't she? Which one is it?" Then without hesitation, he reached over, grabbed onto the elbow of my arm I pointed at, pulled down, yanked out, and cracked my shoulder back into socket. We laughed, hopped down, and went back to what we were doing as if nothing happened. I just had to be a little tender with that arm for the next few hours.

It's important to have friends like this in your life. I know Heath will always be there for me and Heath knows I will always be there for him. There is comfort in knowing I have a friend who understands me. As you will see in a later chapter, Heath was there for me in a way I'll never be able to repay him. But even with the comfort of that friendship, I didn't want many people to know about my issues outside of a very protected circle. Then "The Quarter Incident" happened, and flipped that entire strategy on its head – pardon the impending pun.

Up until this point, I had done a pretty good job of keeping my issues under wraps. Only a small handful of people in the church I work at even knew I had any issues at all. We felt like we let those who *needed* to know, know.

But, once again, I perceived it as a weakness. So anyone outside of that small group was left in the dark. I've always had trust issues because my niceness has been taken advantage of so many times in my life. I think that's one of the factors that made me even more guarded when it came to letting people in on my secrets. Then, one Valentine's Day evening, it became impossible for me to hide it from the people in our church ever again.

Rewind to a month earlier, and the experience that set the stage for what those in attendance that night have all deemed "The Quarter Incident." My concussion issues were sporadic up to this point. It took extreme circumstances for me to pass out, or have a brain episode before this day. But then one morning, I was heading to church early by myself for our worship team sound check. There wasn't anything to differentiate this day from any other Sunday. I walked down the wheelchair ramp off the porch in front of our house on my way to my car. Then the next thing I knew, I was sitting behind the sound booth at the church and we were already halfway through the second service. It's like I blinked my eyes and when they opened, I was in a totally new location. Part of me wanted to react in fear and the other part wanted to daydream about how I had just unlocked this cool new superpower of teleportation.

Apparently, I stepped on a patch of ice on the wheelchair ramp, probably the only ice in the entire state of

Texas. As I was falling, I rolled to try to save from landing on my shoulder. As you can tell from a few paragraphs earlier, both shoulders still have a tendency to dislocate on me from time to time. In the process of trying to save my shoulder, I fell head first off of the *top* of the ramp and onto a wooden pallet on the ground that my wife kept her flowerpots on. As you can imagine, in the process of shattering the wooden pallet, I knocked myself clean out. Who knows how long I laid down there until my wife finally found me laying beside the porch, shaking like a funky-chicken on the ground.

When I finally woke up, she insisted I should stay home. But I was adamant that I still went to church. I don't remember any of the next three hours, but with as many laughs as we have had of other people telling their version of that next three hours; I feel like I should remember it. The rest of this I am telling you comes from other people's recollection. My wife drove me to practice because she knew I shouldn't be driving. During practice, I asked the same questions over and over again. Jack, our Worship Pastor, suggested he should call someone else in to play, to which I would reply "Nah man! I'm good! I'm goooood. Ya. I'm good." He should have called someone else in.

During worship, at one point, he turned around and mouthed to me "What are you playing??" I smiled big at him, nodded, gave him the thumbs up signal, and went back to playing my bass guitar. I thought I was playing the same song as everyone else. Apparently, I wasn't. Thankfully, the soundman muted my bass guitar. I have no idea what I was playing, but they all said I was having a blast playing it. Jack called someone else in to play bass guitar for the second service.

During the second service, they sat me in a chair in the sound booth and told me not to move. Evidently, I kept asking the person running the media computer who they were and introducing myself to them. About every 10 minutes, I would say, "I don't believe we've met. Are you new here?" We laugh at it now, but I'm sure it was annoying her while it was happening.

After that moment, we saw a major spike in my concussion issues. Most times, whenever I get knocked out, it doesn't affect me any more than usual. But every once in a while, I will have one, like this knockout, so bad that it brings considerable change with it. Sometimes it only accelerates an issue I'm already having. Other times it brings a whole new challenge with it, the most recent being seizures I've experienced the past few years when I never had them before.

The new challenge that the slip off the porch triggered was that I periodically lose control of my hands. They will start shaking on their own, similar to the tremors someone with Parkinson's disease has. Sometimes it's small tremors; other times it is shaking so badly my whole arm starts moving too. And it's not isolated to one hand either, although it happens with my left hand almost twice as much as the right. This seems to be triggered mostly by stress or being out in the sun too long. The more stressed I am, or the hotter my body gets, the worse the shaking becomes. Thankfully for me, unlike people with Parkinson's, my tremors will eventually go away. I can't imagine what people have to go through with those happening 24/7. It takes *days* for the cramping to leave my arm after I have one last longer than an hour.

My wife calls my worst knockouts "the personality-altering ones" because she sees a significant change in my personality afterwards. She jokes that she has been married to twenty different men, even though she's only been married once. When I told her I was writing about this incident, she said, "Oh man. That was a bad one. Probably the worst knockout I've seen you have since I've known you. It definitely had the biggest effect on you." Considering I didn't just have a new challenge afterwards – the trembling hands – but I also had a personality change *and* it accelerated an issue I was already dealing with, yes … it was definitely one of the most substantial knockouts I have had.

The biggest impact on my day-to-day life was the increase in passing-out episodes. What was a sporadic event beforehand was now an almost daily occurrence. On many days, I was passing out multiple times. I started having brain episodes on a weekly basis. It was becoming harder and harder to hide my issues from those around me. A little over a month later, we found ourselves forced to make my issues public. Not by choice, but because I passed out in front of the whole church.

Our youth program was doing a fundraiser dinner the night of Valentine's Day. Everyone dressed up. The church was transformed into an old-fashioned Italian restaurant, and the teenagers served the couples Italian meals while they were entertained with live music and comedic "couples" competitions. Towards the end of the night, we always did a fundraiser game called Heads or Tails. It's a twist on the 50/50 concept. You can buy tickets with half the money going towards the youth program and the other half going to the winner. But instead of drawing for a winner, it's the last person standing with a ticket who wins. Every ticket equals a life. Then you have to choose either "heads" or "tails" by putting your hands on your head to signify heads, or your hands on your butt to signify tails, before the coin is flipped. If you guess wrong, then you lose a life and have to give up a ticket. If you run out of tickets, you are eliminated from the game. It's always a fun competition involving strategy and lots of cheating. *Lots* of cheating! It wouldn't be a Dayton Christian Center competition or game if there wasn't cheating of some sort happening. We have a blast at our church.

I emceed the event. So, I'm flipping the coin and fielding the arguments of "not flipping it well enough" by the losers, while the winners are telling them not to be such sore losers; only for them to switch roles the next coin flip. Like I said, we have a lot of fun at our church.

I stood on the stage so people could see me when I flipped the coin. A volunteer picked up the coin and handed it to me after each round. After one of the coin flips, she was pulled away from the game so I bent over to pick up the quarter myself. Big mistake.

I remember bending over, then the next thing I know I'm laying on my back with a crowd of faces around me. The Lead Pastor, David Hilton – a former professional stock contractor himself – jokingly said, "You shoulda seen that joker buck!", making a reference like I just got knocked out after bucking off a bull. I was confused at first, mainly because of David's remark. Then major embarrassment set in as I realized what had transpired. Evidently, as I bent over, I slowly fell forward like a tree cut down, off the stage, and head first onto the floor below. Many there that night have told me my head sounded like a watermelon when it hit the concrete floor. With how close together these two knockouts happened, it could have been this one that garnered a lot of the changes as well; if not a combination of both in such close proximity.

Only a handful of people there knew I had any issues deriving from multiple concussions. To the rest of the people in attendance, it looked like I had just fallen over dead. Apparently, my wife never sounded more like a

Morrison than in that moment. While many people started gathering around me, others ran to her in the back of the sanctuary to tell her I was laid out on the floor not moving. She just hollered out, "Give him some breathin' room! He'll be fine!" If she would have thrown in a, "It's a long way from his heart" comment, she would have made any Morrison patriarch proud. Looking back, we can see why people may have thought she was heartless in the moment. The reality is, she knew I would eventually wake up and be fine. Embarrassed. But fine all the same.

What came out of this incident was the realization that I could no longer hide my issues. As much as I would love to tell people "mind your own business," I couldn't. They just watched one of their executive pastors fall face first off the stage. They had a legitimate concern for my well-being. After a long conversation with my wife, we decided it was time to let people in on the secret and make my struggles public.

Honestly, I hadn't even filled my own dad in yet on what was going on. As bad as that makes me sound, I had legitimate reasoning for it. Around the same time I was increasingly struggling with my brain issues, my mom was diagnosed with adenocarcinoma cancer. A few months later, she died from that cancer. My dad just lost his wife. Then a few weeks later, his mom passed away. Then a couple months after that, his brother-in-law died. My brain issues seemed minute at that point, and I didn't want to add any more stress to him than what he was already shouldering.

As we started becoming more public with my struggles, something happened I never expected. More of my friends started opening up to me, privately, about their own concussion issues. Their wives commented to us about how relieved they were to see their husbands finally be able to talk to someone about it. I realized there were a lot more people going through what I was going through, and that I wasn't alone. It may not be on the same scale or similar symptoms, but it was still things that were affecting their day-to-day lives. By sharing my problems even more publicly, I may be able to help others … people I wouldn't have reached before. Even if it's just one person, it is worth it.

So as hard as it is to open myself up – and further peel back the curtains of my glass house – I *have* to talk about what happened in this next chapter.

CHAPTER 12

WHEN I THOUGHT I HAD ONLY ONE OPTION

Nick's daughter, Gracie (10), using a bow-target as a flotation device to get around their neighborhood during Hurricane Harvey in 2017. She is floating over what is usually the county road into their property.

How far was I from any oceans growing up? My dad's ranch in Potato Creek, South Dakota, is less than seven miles from North America's Pole of Inaccessibility. Each continent's Pole of Inaccessibility marks the location on that continent that is the furthest from any ocean or coastline in every direction, with this marker being over 1,000 miles from the nearest coastline. So, I grew up only seven miles away from being, literally, the farthest from any ocean as you can possibly be across all of Canada, Mexico, and the United States. It's safe to say, we certainly didn't have any hurricanes during my childhood.

While I may not have lived through any hurricanes then, we were definitely baptised into them almost immediately upon moving to Texas. After living there for only one month, we found ourselves serving food in a shelter to many of the estimated 200,000 evacuees who fled to Houston from New Orleans during Hurricane Katrina. Less than a month after that, we were evacuated from our own home, with a three-month-old baby in tow, due to Hurricane Rita. Since then, we have ridden out direct impacts from Hurricane Ike, Hurricane Harvey, and Hurricane Beryl, as well as multiple tropical storms scattered throughout the years. None impacted us more, personally, than Hurricane Harvey in 2017.

Two things made Harvey very unique. First was how quickly it developed while in the gulf, growing from a minor Tropical Depression into a Tropical Storm, then

Category-4 Hurricane, all within 40 hours. Most people in the area didn't even know a storm was coming until roughly twelve hours before it made landfall.

The other thing that made it unique is where most hurricanes pass through within a few hours, Harvey stalled in one place for *four days*, slamming the same area over and over again. Those days felt like *weeks* to those of us enduring the storm.

Harvey originally made landfall in the Rockport area, devastating entire towns. It bounced back into the gulf to regain strength before hitting the Houston area hours later. A high-pressure system moving from the north sandwiched the hurricane against the high-pressure system moving from the south that was pushing it inland. Sitting stalled – half in the ocean, half on land – as the storm rotated, it picked up moisture from the ocean and continually dumped it inland.

Thirty-three trillion gallons of water. That's how much estimated rain Hurricane Harvey dumped during a storm that seemed like it would never end. At the time of writing this book, it's the most rainfall ever recorded in US history, with enough water to fill over 50 million Olympic-sized swimming pools. It's calculated, according to the *Atlantic Magazine*, that over 275 trillion pounds of water fell from the sky during this storm. That is roughly 77% of the landmass of Mount Everest! Chris Milliner, from NASA's Jet Propulsion Laboratory, estimated that the weight of that much water physically warped the Earth's crust in the Houston, Texas, area, causing it to sink around 2 centimeters![1]

Our house, during this time, was located about 45 miles west of Houston in Dayton, Texas. We were in the middle of what is considered the "dirty side" of the storm. This is the northwest side of a hurricane that rotates up from the ocean, having the most water contained within its clouds. The dirty side is considered the most dangerous part of a hurricane because it typically gets the most storm surge, wind speed, rainfall, and tornadoes. What Harvey lacked in wind speed, compared to other hurricanes I have ridden-out, it made up for in rain. I have never lived through that much rainfall in my life and hope to never live through it again.

I tried staying up the whole night before to watch the storm path on the news, even though it was a very small chance we would be in its path. By 4 AM, it looked like we would miss the majority of the storm, other than a little rain. So, I went to bed, and my wife started her shift keeping an eye on the storm. The yard was completely dry at this point. During the next hour, the storm "skipped" along the coast and made landfall farther east than expected. At 5 AM, my wife woke me up as a

1. Madrigal, Alexis C. "Harvey Pushed the Earth's Crust down by 2 Centimeters." *The Atlantic*, Atlantic Media Company, 5 Sept. 2017, www.theatlantic.com/technology/archive/2017/09/hurricane-harvey-deformed-the-earths-crust-around-houston/538866/.

torrential downpour was just beginning. We went outside to double-check that the vehicles were on the highest ground of our property. The water was already ankle-deep in our yard. We then tied down everything that was loose as the water was rising more rapidly. The water rose at such a rate that we had friends who woke up around this time, and when they stood out of bed, they were already standing in thigh-deep water throughout their entire house. Thankfully, we were living in a double-wide trailer at this time, so the water would have to rise quite a bit more to get into our home.

It was undoubtedly the hardest rainstorm I had ever seen in my life. The best way I could visually describe it is if you are standing under one of those big buckets in the kids' area of a water park as it tips over. But this bucket of water was nonstop. By 7:00 AM, any land or roads in our neighborhood were completely hidden by water. By 8:00 AM, the water was already over waist-deep in our yard. The rain never stopped for almost four days. It would slow down to a normal hard rain, but then come back in a wave of full-force for about 30 minutes every two hours.

Our house never flooded outright. Water got right up to the doorway, but never broke into the home. The house was located on the highest area of our property, and being a double-wide mobile home meant it was up off the ground on blocks as well. Each reprieve of lighter rain would give the water a chance to recede just enough before the next wave of full-force rain began again, bringing water right up to the doorstep, but not inside, each time.

Many of our neighbors were evacuated by boat within the first couple of days. We chose to stay behind to try and prevent water from getting in the house if the flood ever breached our doorstep. We also promised to keep an eye on neighbors' houses, as looters were already trying to take advantage of people in the middle of a crisis. I had to chase off looters – at gunpoint – on two separate occasions.

Our storage shed sat in water for the majority of the storm. Beforehand we stacked everything that was in plastic tubs first. Then, about four feet up, we placed the cardboard boxes, with our most valuable keepsakes on top of those. So, we figured anything of value in storage should be fine. On the third day of the storm, we were getting stir crazy. So, during one of the regular rain spells, we opened the shed to assess any damage. It was a total mess. The water rose high enough to soak the cardboard boxes, which eventually collapsed. The most valuable keepsakes fell into the water, and were held underwater by the boxes that tumbled over them. We lost so many things. Most of my old bull riding equipment, pictures, all of our baby keepsakes, and my stack of back numbers – one of the things rodeo athletes collect to remember all of the big rodeos they competed at throughout their entire career – were a few of the items that were completely ruined.

The hardest for me to swallow was when I found the letters my mom had written me right before she died. She couldn't speak the final few days, so she wrote us very heartfelt letters. I was never man enough to read them yet, as she had only passed a few years earlier, but planned to when I could finally face them. The realization that I never read her last dying words to me, that were now so soaked that the ink had run off of them, absolutely broke me.

The fourth morning of the storm, my wife and I took off wading toward a friend's house a couple miles away to retrieve their kayak. Since I had been watching the news in the days leading up to the storm, we had stocked up on bottled water and non-perishables in preparation just in case. Others in our neighborhood, who had not yet been evacuated, were running out of food and water. Our plan was to load the kayak with bottled water and canned food to pull around the neighborhood to give to those who needed it.

On our way to retrieve the kayak, we were walking along the raised-up county roads that ran through our neighborhood. Even at that height, we were still in thigh deep water. About a mile into our walk, we felt this sudden surge in the water that almost knocked both of us to the ground. There was now a very strong current that made it hard to keep our feet under us. We could tell the water was moving somewhere in a hurry. By the time we walked the next mile, retrieved the kayak, and started working our way back towards our house, the very roads we were walking on, in thigh-deep water moments earlier, were now exposed.

The water in our neighborhood was previously being held-up by elevated train tracks, without enough culverts for drainage along the embankment to keep up with the amount of water dumping from the skies. Eventually, about three-quarters of a mile directly behind our house, the sheer pressure of the water opened a wide breach in the embankment as the dirt under the tracks collapsed. This caused an enormous rush of water out of our neighborhood. By the time we got back to our house, the water in our yard was now only around knee-deep. By that afternoon, there were even patches of grass showing.

When the embankment breached, the water of the neighborhood all rushed through our section, with a lot of it going under and around our home. I figured, when I saw large sections of missing skirting from around the bottom of the house, it was because of the force of the water. Since we were away from the house when it happened, we didn't know that debris from people's porches that had been ripped by the rushing water, and other loose items laying around our neighbors' yards, accompanied that surge of water through our place.

That debris slammed against the side of our home and tore up the entire underbelly of our house. We found out later, when moving that house off the property, that we were extremely fortunate. We stayed living in that home for months not knowing the entire home shifted on the blocks. It was one small gust of wind away from crashing off those blocks.

The rain finally stopped later that afternoon. But we were also bracing for what was determined to be an even harder blow over the next two to three days. Harvey had moved back into the Gulf and was gaining strength for another landfall. The projected pattern for the new path had it coming directly over top of us. Thankfully for us, but not for the Beaumont area, the storm took another unexpected turn east and made landfall on the Texas/Louisiana border. After what we had already been through, if Harvey would have stayed its course, I don't think our area could have handled another storm surge.

Companies immediately went to work fixing infrastructure. This was only a temporary reprieve, though. The hurricane rain filled Lake Livingston and Lake Conroe to dangerous levels. To prevent breaches of their own, water was released from their dams. All of that water had to go somewhere, flooding the area spreading from Kingwood to Liberty. The railroad embankment by our house was fixed almost immediately, so when this new rush of water came, it put our neighborhood under water once again. The biggest problem was, we didn't know we had extensive damage under our home. So when *this* water flooded our neighborhood, even though water never visibly entered the house, it was coming up from underneath the house. Water was seeping into our subfloors and walls. It was slowly destroying our home without our knowledge.

Having a church full of men with boats came in very handy. They were bonafide heroes during and after the storm. These men were going into neighborhoods with air-boats, bringing entire families out of their homes. They would then transport them to other men waiting in pontoon boats or fishing boats, who motored those people to higher ground where even *more* men were waiting with jacked-up trucks to drive them to shelters. Once they knew the people in the area were safe, they started saving animals. They were "cowboying" from their boats, roping as many animals as they could find, tying them to the side of the boat, then transporting them alongside the boat to higher ground. These men saved hundreds of cattle, horses, deer, hogs … whatever animals that needed saving. They found many of the animals standing on their toes, against a tree limb, or the top of a panel, trying to keep their head above water; exhausted from trying to survive the previous days.

When the storm had finally passed, it now became a giant effort of cleaning up the mess. We knew numerous people whose houses flooded. In the Texas heat, it's a race against time to get the wet areas out of the house as quickly as possible. Potentially deadly black mold will form in those wet areas, rendering a home uninhabitable. All walls and floors where water sat had to be cut out and replaced. Once again our church family stepped up. Numerous volunteers come forward to help the families repair their damage. We hit the ground running before the storm had even fully passed over Louisiana. While roads were still flooded in some areas, we focused on the areas available to us first and worked our way to those homes once we could get to them.

The sheer carnage of debris stacked outside of homes made our entire area look like a war zone for the next couple months.

I worked to coordinate the effort the best I could, sending groups of volunteers to every corner of the surrounding area. While my wife and kids worked alongside me in a church member's home, ripping out their subfloors and cutting out their walls, I was also constantly on my phone, making sure every affected home had people in them doing the same. If anyone knew of someone else who needed help, they would call me. I would then call and check on our volunteers to see who we could send to those locations. We were so stretched thin that in some homes, only one or two volunteers cleared those homes out all by themselves. Others in the church were cooking food and feeding all of our workers. Dozens of friends from all over the country came to help in the effort. We had them scattered, staying with people from the church whose houses didn't get damaged. It was truly a full team effort.

We left before the sun rose and returned well after dark every day. My wife and I were so focused on everyone else's homes, we never thought to thoroughly inspect ours. This proved to be a monumental mistake. Other than a section of the ceiling in the guest bathroom that fell during the heavy rains, we seemed to be okay. We taped off that area and decided we would work on it after everyone else's homes were taken care of first. More than a week into our cleanup process, I was walking across our kitchen one morning, and stepped on an area where you could feel the floor go "squishy soft." One of the friends staying at our house crawled underneath, and what he found was disheartening to say the least. Further inspection would prove devastating.

Remember when that train-track embankment broke and all the water/debris rushed under our house? This is when we found the extent of that damage. Holes were ripped through our AC vents. The ductwork was ripped completely away from the house, which we didn't notice because we had been without power during most of this time. Insulation was hanging everywhere. But the worst part was the openings torn into the thick black plastic that separated the insulation from the subfloors. The insulation acted like a wick and soaked water up. As the water from the second flooding sat against the bottom of the house, it seeped into the holes in the plastic. Water filled up the entirety of the black plastic across the whole house, and trapped it against the subfloors. That water then sat for over a week and a half, slowly soaking through. While we didn't officially flood during the hurricane itself, we flooded slowly over the course of two weeks. Within days of discovering this, water started seeping through the carpets across the entire home.

Black mold had already started forming on the ceiling throughout the house. The force of the water during the rain caused damage to the roof, leaking water onto the ceiling. We were now seeing damage from above and below. One quick look inside the walls showed that water was leaking down the walls as well, forming black mold all up and down the inside of both the interior and exterior walls of the house. One of our friends staying with us was a contractor. He assessed the damage and said we were more than likely looking at a total loss on the house. The cost to replace the roof, walls, and subfloors damaged from the water would cost more than what our double-wide trailer house was worth. Regardless, we still had other people's homes to take care of first. Ours could wait.

When everyone else's houses were in order, we shifted attention to our home. We finally let people know we were dealing with something ourselves as well, and it was amazing to see the response. So many people showed up that we were able to work on most of our house in one day. We took out all of the carpet, all of the tiling, and all of the linoleum flooring to expose the subfloors. We cut out sections of most of the walls. Black mold was *everywhere*. The black mold had already grown so thick on one side of the house that we trapped it off with thick plastic and quarantined it from the rest of the home.

We had a second and third opinion look at our house over the next few days and they all concurred that our house was a total loss. I figured this shouldn't be a problem as both insurance and FEMA would help us with this situation, especially with it being deemed "totaled" by three separate contractors. I couldn't have been more wrong. I filed with our insurance and tried to file online with FEMA. Both times I filed with FEMA, I was denied immediately because we didn't have water breach the house during the storm, and they weren't covering roof damage; only flooding.

That was okay, though, because I knew we had full-total coverage on our home, and the check from the insurance for a totaled house would pay off what we still owed, and would leave enough left over to put a down payment on a new one. After our insurance sent an adjuster, I finally got a letter from them. They claimed that, while they agree the house is totaled, they think most of the damage is from flooding not from roof damage. Since they don't cover floods, they offered only $1,000 in total for our damage. But since our deductible was $1,000, it offset the deductible and "you won't have to pay a deductible if you make another claim from another storm this year."

That was their fancy way of saying they weren't sending us any money.

I was livid. I immediately called our insurance to talk to someone. They stated that it couldn't be proven the roof damage was from *this* storm, because there was a small hailstorm in our county three months earlier and we never sent a claim for the hailstorm – which we didn't claim because that storm was on the other side of the county and never came close to our home. Therefore, they are not liable for any damages done to the house, but are doing us a "favor" by still wiping out our deductible for any *new* damages the rest of the year. You have to love insurances.

So now, after hanging up the phone with the insurance adjuster, I am standing by myself in our home, looking at cut out walls, bare subfloors, and plastic-patched ceiling holes. I'm realizing I have a total loss on a home without even close to enough money saved to fix it or buy a new one. Insurance is claiming it's flood damage, not ceiling damage, so they can't cover it. FEMA is claiming it's ceiling damage, not flood damage, so they can't cover it.

I needed to let off some steam. There was a section in the kitchen where we hadn't yet started removing the walls. We planned to with friends later that weekend. I decided to start cutting that section out by myself, because the idea of destroying walls sounded like a good outlet for the anger I was feeling.

As I cut the first part out, I encountered an area of wall behind it that had the sheetrock doubled-thick and was backed up against the cupboards in the guest bathroom on the other side. I slowly cut along the wall and reached in to tear the wall section out. I'm mad. I'm not worried about safety. I just want to rip something up to get rid of my anger. I have no mask, no protective-glasses, and am not wearing any gloves. I reached in-between the doubled sheetrock with my fingers and worked them across to get a good hold on that section. In one big motion to rip the wall, my hands slid off of their grip and I fell backwards onto my butt. My fingers were covered in black slime. I just found a large pocket of thick black mold. Not only did I find it, but I put my hands all over it and opened up the spores by disturbing them.

I would find out later that heavy exposure to black mold can accelerate symptoms of a brain injury. I didn't know this at the time or else I wouldn't have been anywhere near the black mold. According to research, black mold can exacerbate beta spindles, high-frequency brainwave bursts that make the repercussions of brain injuries worse.[2] My exposure to black mold, I believe, intensified my sensitivity to cognitive stimuli. Because of the toxins I inhaled, my feelings of hopelessness and desperation

2. "Mold Brain Impact." *Omni Neurofeedback*, 18 Dec. 2024, https://omnineurofeedback.com/blog/f/mold-brain-impact#:~:text=Recovering%20from%20a%20head%20injury,brain%20function%20and%20impaired%20recovery.

amplified so that the voice of reason in my head was temporarily silenced.

I decided to get in the shower to cool off. This is when things turned really dark. In the shower, I started to hallucinate, seeing big bugs flying all around my head. Then I started to think about our house. Even more I started to focus on what a loser I was. I failed in my bull riding career. I failed in college. Now I failed in protecting my family and giving them a home. I was helpless. There was nothing I could do. I started beating myself up in my mind with all of my mistakes and shortcomings.

But then a solution came to mind. I remembered Ivy had taken out a life insurance policy on me a couple years earlier. If I ended my life, she could cash that policy in and the family could get a new home. While it wasn't ideal, it felt like my only option at the time. The more I thought about it, the more it made sense. Sure, my family would miss me. But then Ivy could remarry down the road and have someone in her life she didn't have to stress over as much as she does me. Plus I could donate my brain to research and do far more to help the concussion community as a dead man than I ever could alive. I was convinced this was my only option.

I stepped out of the shower, dried off, and got dressed in nice clothes as I didn't want to be found naked. Through tears I wrote a heartfelt good-bye letter to my wife and one to each of my kids, hoping to help them understand why I was doing what I was doing. I wrote a note explaining that I wanted my brain donated for research. I then sent my wife a simple text that read, "Don't let the kids come in the house when you get home." I grabbed my Smith & Wesson Extended Barrel .357 Magnum pistol, loaded it, and sat down in the shower. Even then I was reasoning that by doing it in the shower, it would leave for an easier cleanup for everyone else.

I've always had this inner voice that would be stronger than any of my urges to harm myself prior to this. Some silly thought would enter my head of suicide, and I would simply tell myself, "That's idiotic. Don't do it," and move on. Sometimes it was harder than others, but that inner voice always won. I knew by this point, it was the concussions talking. But this instance was different. This time my brain was so convinced this was the only option, that my inner voice was almost drowned out completely. Almost. It became this struggle as I *knew* this was something I shouldn't do, yet I was convinced I *had* to do it.

I checked the pistol one more time to make sure it was loaded. I positioned the pistol around in my mouth to try and find an angle where I knew it would kill me, yet leave enough brain for research. I decided I didn't want to botch this up … my brain had convinced me I was such a complete loser that I couldn't even do this right. So I felt around my chest to find the strongest heartbeat and placed the barrel of the pistol there. Tears were streaming down my face. It was this inward turmoil I was facing as my head is telling me I have to do this or my family won't have a house. But my heart is telling me, "You know you don't want to do this." I fought off the urge to back out. If I had to do this, now would have to be the time. "*Besides, I already sent Ivy the text. She knows something is up. If I don't follow through with this, will she see me as a loser now too? No. I have to do this now.*"

Memories flooded my head. Thoughts circled in my mind. Would people be proud of the life I led up to this moment or disappointed in me that it ended this way? Would all of my years of work go out the window with this one decision? Will people ever understand why I did it? That all didn't matter now. The only thing that mattered was getting my family a new house, and my brain was convinced this was the only way to accomplish that.

So there I sat on the floor of our walk-in shower. My back leaned against the wall, my legs straight out in front of me, soaking wet from the water droplets still lingering around the drain from my shower only moments earlier. One hand held the barrel of a gun to my chest, the other with the thumb on the trigger. While I never felt at peace with it, I knew it was what I needed to do.

My heart was racing. I was breathing heavily. I closed my eyes through their tears and tried to slow my breathing. I took one deep breath, tensed my entire body, squinted my eyes, and pulled the trigger.

Chapter 13

The 15 Minute Rule

Nick (32) speaking to a large group of student athletes and their parents at the Spillane Middle School Champions Breakfast. Photo courtesy of Wes Foster

CLICK

In the resounding silence of my shower, the only sound was that which a gun makes whenever the hammer strikes air after the trigger is pulled with an empty chamber. Surely I wasn't such a failure that I had forgotten to load the gun first? So I checked. All six chambers of the revolver's cylinder were filled with a bullet. The bullet that was supposed to fire – that was destined to be my end – had a notch on the primer cap where the hammer hit it, yet the bullet never fired. I let out a muffled squeal and dropped the gun, my face falling into my hands crying. This break in my emotions was *just enough* of a sliver of hope to let my inner voice finally be heard.

My mind was still convinced this was the only thing I could do to get my family a new house. But, for the first time since I opened that pocket of black mold spores, my inner voice had an equally assertive conviction that it wasn't worth it. I was at a stalemate.

I didn't want to call anyone because most people would just say, "You don't want to do this." I *know* I don't want to do this. The only person that I knew would be able to see it in the same light would be someone else who has had close to as many concussions as me. So I called one of my closest friends, who I mentioned earlier, Heath Ford. While Heath hadn't dealt with this exact situation, I knew he could speak my language due to the amount of concussions he has endured himself.

So we talked. I won't go over the details of our conversation in this book, because that's private. But he got my mind to go to another place. He got my concentration off wanting to kill myself. My brain couldn't convince me it was the only option anymore. To Heath, it may not have been that big of a conversation. But to me, it was exactly what I needed at that moment. The black mold in my system was wearing off, the emotions were settling, and I was starting to think clearly again. We hung up the phone, I put the gun away, and then waited on the bed for my wife to get home. Even though I sent her a follow-up text saying I was okay, I also knew she would be panicking from the text I sent earlier.

I'm going to take a minute away from telling the story to really focus on this for a second. You may be the person dealing with these thoughts. You may be the person who has sat on your bathroom shower floor convinced that suicide is your only option. You need to understand that there is *way* more to life than ending it at that moment. I know it's hard when that moment approaches. But you have to hold fast to the positives in your life – your loved ones and your future. Cling to them with every part of your inner being. You *need* a friend you can call who can speak your language and encourage you out of that situation. You *must* get your mindset out of that dark place. If not, it will consume you to where you believe there is no other option.

I can relate because I've been there. If you've never been in that situation, it's hard to comprehend what that person is going through. We try to justify things in our minds, but the reality is you don't know what you don't know. My hope in sharing this extremely difficult story is so that you can walk through the mindset of a person going through that situation. Maybe it will help you to better understand someone close to you so you can help them if ever faced with this. Maybe it's the beginning of the closure you needed to answer the question of "Why?" that has been boring into your soul ever since a loved one close to you, who struggled with concussion issues, took their own life. You *need* to know that their brain convinced them they were doing something they were *supposed* to do.

I'm certain of this because, two years later, I would attempt suicide again. This time I didn't have black mold influencing me, but it was rather brought on by the vituperate actions of other individuals. I originally wrote an entire chapter about it for later in the book, but ultimately decided to delete that chapter. While I was being careful of what I wrote or omitted, it was becoming impossible to write the details leading up to that second suicide attempt without permanently tarnishing the reputation of others. I left out names, but those close to me are smart enough to connect the dots to figure out who I was talking about. Regardless of whether the people involved deserve ridicule is not the point. It doesn't align with my purpose for writing this book. That is not me, nor my heart. I have forgiven those who took it too far, although I now keep them at a considerable arm's length. My concussion struggles don't afford me to hold bitterness towards them. But it also required me cutting people completely out of my circle who showed no desire to change from continually being divisive.

The biggest takeaway from my second suicide attempt, two years later, was how calm I was compared to the first time. My mind was once again convinced I would be doing a favor to everyone else around me, as it was maliciously told to me how worthless a human being I am just a couple hours earlier. There was no internal fight, but an eerie peace in my mind. It was like my brain had added it to a checklist of chores I must do when I get home. It was late in the evening when I pulled into the driveway. I let the dogs out back to run, filled their dog food and water bowls, then grabbed the pistol and headed into the backyard to join the dogs. I don't know what possessed me to grab the same bullet that had misfired the first time, but I felt like it would be poetic if that bullet was the one to finish the deed. Once again, I was calm this entire time. There was no battle with an inner voice like before. I didn't want the bullet to go through me and possibly enter the house, so I grabbed a pool chair to lay on and dragged it out into a dark area of the yard, far away from the home. I sat on the chair, and with no second guessing, in one swift motion, I lifted the gun to the side of my head and pulled the trigger.

CLICK

Again?! I walked into light, cascading over the fence from a telephone pole in our front yard, to look at the bullet. Sure enough, the same bullet had a *second* notch where the hammer hit it. Finally, a voice of reason pushed through. I called out to God and screamed, "*What do you want from me?!*" I decided that if God was not done with me, then He was preventing that bullet from firing. If it was just happening by chance, then it must be a faulty bullet. So, I made a deal. I would fire the same bullet into the ground, and if it fired, then I knew my entire purpose in life moving forward would be to use what I've been dealing with to hopefully prevent it in others. If it didn't fire, then I would take that as a sign that I was supposed to find another way to end my life.

I spun the cylinder so that bullet would be the next to fire, pointed the gun to the ground, and pulled the trigger. The power from the .357 bullet firing out of the barrel actually caught me by surprise. I had my answer.

As dark as that night was, it was one of the biggest turning points in my life. Up until that day, I had put far too much weight in what other people thought about me. I like to say, "I have enough of my dad in me that I don't mind ticking people off, but enough of my mom in me that it bothers me when I do." If I ever felt I upset someone, then I would toil over it trying to think of how I could make it right. I would lose sleep playing the scenario that unfolded over and over again in my mind.

Like anything I've struggled with in the past, I had to find a way to change my mindset. That meant no longer caring about people's opinions, because of how deeply that infected my mind. A change like that doesn't happen naturally. It's an easy battle on some days, and a constant war on others. But I've learned how to win those battles more as time has progressed. If someone doesn't like me, that's their loss. I now only care what God, my wife, and my kids think about me. This has unfettered me from the unnecessary pressure I used to hang over myself to accommodate others. After that night, and for the first time in my life, I was finally making my health my first priority.

But before any of that breakthrough occurred, we have to come back to the original timeline, and the first time I attempted suicide. It was the darkest place I had ever been. On the day of my first suicide attempt, when I wasn't strong enough, God said, "I'm not done with you yet," and stepped in.

When my wife got home she made a statement that turned my entire mindset around. One statement. "I would rather live in a cardboard box with you still here than in a mansion without you." It made me realize that no matter what, I always have my family. I couldn't do that to them – put them through what they would have endured in the days, even years, after my moment of weakness. I may not have thought of those consequences when I was in my darkest moment, but the threat of bringing that pain to my family helps keep me focused to not let myself get to that place again.

Now that I know where my darkest place dwells, I know my limits. Have suicidal thoughts tried entering my mind since then? Yes, almost every time I get into a depressive state. I have to *choose* to not entertain them, something easier said than done at times. I let the thoughts go in one ear and out the other, not giving them a chance to take any root in my mind. If those thoughts try to stick around, I think about that statement. "I would rather live in a cardboard box with you still here than in a mansion without you."

My wife and I sat on our bed talking. She was crying. I was feeling embarrassed more than anything else. The totaled house, no insurance coverage, no FEMA assistance, our savings and bank accounts wiped clean trying to fix what we could – none of that mattered. What mattered was that I had a wife who loved me, despite what flaws she married into. I had two kids who looked up to me, learning from my every move. The house may be totaled, with black mold throughout every corner, but at least it's a roof over our heads. We may be starting completely over at zero, but we're doing it together.

We still had around $100,000 owed on the house/property. We couldn't move out of this situation until we paid it off and saved up enough money to put a down payment on a new home. We were in it for the long haul, as a family. Looking back, I'm amazed at how much our kids were troopers through this time. A quarter of the house was quarantined off with thick plastic because the black mold was too dense in those areas. During the hottest days, I watched mold physically growing on the walls, like some scene out of a scary movie.

If we are going to live in a house with cut out walls and only subfloors for our foreseeable future, we are going to make the best out of it. *If you aren't having fun, make your own fun.* So we bought sidewalk chalk and told the kids to "have at it." Not every kid gets to draw all over their house without repercussions. One of my favorite memories was a big circle the kids drew in the middle of the living room, where we played old-school marbles almost every night.

My dad taught us to never quit, no matter the circumstances. One night, while laying in bed praying over our situation, I remembered a rule I had invented for myself when riding bulls: the 15 Minute Rule. Not only would that rule be a major turning point in this situation, it has become a staple of my very being ever since.

To ride bulls successfully, you have to learn to "hate the ground." What I mean by that is you have to despise bucking off. If not, you'll check out at the first sign of getting in trouble on a bull, rather than make the split-second decision to attempt to recover and continue. As the saying goes, "Bull riding is 10% physical and 90% mental." The biggest battle when riding bulls is the confidence in your mind.

My brother used to say that he could tell if I was going to ride my bull or not, simply by my body language as I was sliding up on my rope to nod my head. If I lacked confidence, I made a lot of mistakes. If I had my mind made up I wasn't bucking off, there wasn't a bull that could throw me. It's easy to say, "Well, there ya go! Always have your mind made up that you're not bucking off then!" That is the *most* "easier said than done" thing I've ever faced in my life.

I would get streaky. I was emotional in my passion for riding bulls. Cover a bull, and I was filled with excitement. I would usually go on a streak of riding the next few bulls in a row solely off of that confidence. Buck off of a bull, and I was as mad as a hornet's nest. I would stew on it and think about it the entire drive to the next rodeo. Then I would buck off every bull I got on for the next couple of weeks. I had to come up with something that could break this cycle mentally. That's when I invented the 15 Minute Rule.

It was simple. I had fifteen minutes, buck off or ride, to have my emotional response, whether that was elation for making the 8-seconds or a pity-party for bucking off. Fifteen minutes. After that, it was self-evaluation time, when no more emotional response was allowed. I asked myself three questions after every bull I got on: "What did I do right? What did I do wrong? What can I improve on?" Buck off or ride, I always had something to reflect on that I did right, wrong, and an area for improvement. Sometimes the only thing I did right was nod my head for them to open the gate, but I always found something positive at least. Implementing this rule personally into my bull riding gave me a massive surge in my riding percentage. I believe the 15 Minute Rule was a big contributing factor to why I saw such an increase in my riding abilities the last couple years of my career.

So as I'm laying in bed praying about our circumstance, the 15 Minute Rule came back into my memory. How can I implement that into my current situation at hand? I laid there and completely revamped the rule to be more about circumstances in my life, rather than simply my mindset after bucking off or riding a bull. It is now a marquee rule for me anytime something drastic happens.

Fifteen minutes isn't a hard-set time, because some circumstances take longer than a quick fifteen minutes to process what is even going on. How long that takes is fully predicated on how serious the moment is, or how long it takes for the person to emotionally handle what has just happened to them. Sometimes it's the same day. Sometimes it takes a few days, or even a week. But at some point, a person reaches a moment when they have to stop wallowing in pity over their circumstances, and decide it's time to move forward.

In this instance, others you will read about later, and some circumstances that didn't even make this book, I had to eventually make the decision that my fifteen minutes was up. What has happened, happened. I can't control that. What I *can* control is my *attitude* and my *motivation* moving forward. What went right? What went wrong? What can I improve on?

Why is it so important to focus on these three questions?

First question: "What went right?" In most devastating circumstances, nothing went right, but there are always some positives I can focus on. Fixating on the negatives of a situation forces that person's mind to only see negative results. Every word said and every action taken are now funneled through that filter of negativity. Quickly that person will find themselves lacking any positive progression because they only see the negative side of everything surrounding their situation. Focusing on the positives, *despite* the negative circumstances surrounding them during that time, helps the brain to filter positive reinforcement. If there is no light at the end of a tunnel, discouragement begins to fester that there is no hope in sight. Even if it is the slightest dot of light peeking through at the farthest reaches of the tunnel, that tiny dot of positivity becomes a beacon to focus on as the light broadens and the darkness wanes with every step closer to a breakthrough.

Second question: "What went wrong?" It's extremely naive for a person to go through something negative in their life and think it's a 100% attack on them and not at all a result of anything they had done leading up to it. Listen, sometimes life happens. Having a house totaled by a hurricane happens. Nothing we had done leading up to that, with our knowledge at that time, could have prevented it. But sitting on the knowledge we learned from that tragedy and still doing nothing with it leaves no free-pass for excuses if it ever happened again. You better believe I know more of the fine print in my insurance policies moving forward and know to check small signs of water-leakage around the house during a storm. What we learned during Hurricane Harvey saved our house when flooding from Tropical Storm Imelda hit us almost exactly two years to the day later.

But not all negatives in our life are solely by chance. Only the most narcissistic of people think they never do wrong and all circumstances that come their way are always the result of other people's actions. It's important to learn from our mistakes, and admit to ourselves when we have performed – either consciously or sub-consciously – actions leading up to the tragedy that could have been avoided. "Did the way I treat people or talk to people have anything to do with what happened?" "Did my attitude or actions lead to this failure?" If a person keeps getting the same negative circumstance, there's a pretty good chance there is an action or attitude flaw they need to address that keeps nurturing a negative result.

Third question: "What can I improve on?" The second question almost always leads to an answer for the third question. It's one thing to admit you may have made mistakes. It's another thing to work towards improvement in those areas. Unless a person can honestly find their mistakes, admit their wrongs, and work towards improving on those faults moving forward, they will repeatedly find themselves right back in the same failures or negative circumstances. There is no improvement without *seeking* improvement first.

Laying there in bed that night, remapping The 15 Minute Rule, my whole heart switched from focusing on the circumstance to focusing on finding a solution. My fifteen minutes were up. What could I do moving forward? I couldn't leave my wife and kids in this gutted-out home full of black mold. I had a target goal: at least $125,000. That's what it would take to pay off the current loan and have enough for a down payment on a new loan. How long it took to come up with that money was irrelevant. I couldn't come up with $125,000 if I didn't come up with $1 first.

I fully leaned into a statement that I had heard a friend say a couple months earlier: "Work like it depends on you. Pray like it depends on God." That was my motto I lived by through this entire situation. Anytime people would ask what my plan was, I would only reply, "Work like it depends on me. Pray like it depends on God."

I can pray for God to work miracles, which it was going to take a pretty big miracle to get out of this house. But faith without works is dead. I can be a boat asking God to give me direction, and God is sitting there yanking back and forth on my steering wheel, but if I'm still sitting back at the boat ramp, tied to the dock; no amount of steering is going to tell my boat where to go. The boat has to be moving forward for that direction to take place.

So I focused all of my attention on two things: my faith in God performing a miracle and working as hard as I possibly could to pay for it myself.

A few months before Hurricane Harvey had hit, my wife and I had joined a new business. One of my good friends asked to come to our house and talk with us. He is an *exceptional* musician, so I thought he was coming to tell me he was finally going full-time on the road as a musician and wanted me to be his bass player. Nope. He wanted to tell us about a new Multi-Level-Marketing (MLM) company they were a part of. At first, I couldn't hold back laughing at his proposal. Then we prayed about it and had a peace about joining; if anything just to support this friend and his wife.

Let me stop all of you MLM vultures right there. Don't come up to my merch table after a show, all excited after finding out this fact and try pitching me your amazing MLM company. I'm sure it's great. You have to know, I'm a one-trick pony. I did my time. My wife and I always pray that God not only guides our steps, but He also guides our *stops*. In high school, I always said I didn't want to work around teenagers or live in Texas. At 22 years old, I found myself living in Texas leading hundreds of teenagers – and loving it. Now I tell God, "I don't want to live in Hawaii or own a Lamborghini." So far He has not taken the bait, and has fulfilled both of those requests. That being said, will I ever do a company like this again? I'll never say never with God, but … don't hold your breath.

Work like it depends on me. Pray like it depends on God. Nothing about multi-level marketing was enticing to me. *Nothing*. The idea of going into people's homes and trying to sell them a product was agonizing to me. But I was facing an immovable situation, and here is an opportunity to work hard on my end to help towards fixing it. So that's what I did. I went to work telling people about this new company. Early on, I was faced with a lot of disappointment … a lot of getting laughed at. I don't blame them because that was my natural response too. After leaving houses empty handed, I would just repeat the phrase, "Work like it depends on me. Pray like it depends on God," over and over again on my drive home. I would wake up the next morning, make a few phone calls for opportunities to give my presentation, then go to work with my normal job at the church. Later that evening, after work, I would drive to another person's house or jump on a Zoom call and give the pitch again. Wash, rinse, repeat. Work like it depends on me. Pray like it depends on God.

Eventually a spark started. We finally had a small team of around a dozen people under us. We started seeing the first bit of money coming in. A $50 check wasn't going to get us out of the house, but it was a start. We focused on building those teams under us. I may not like going into homes to sell a product, but give me a team of people to lead and I will *thrive* in leadership. More people started joining the team. A $50 check turned into one for $100, then $1,000, then $2,500, then $10,000. Through the hard work of people in Tennessee, Montana, Colorado, Texas, Florida, Nevada, Alabama, Mississippi, Kansas, Missouri, Arkansas, and Nebraska, that team started taking off. We watched as our business grew, in less than two months, from around a dozen people to over 2,500 in the blink of an eye. And to over 7,500 the following year.

Work like it depends on me. Pray like it depends on God. His hand was as evident in that business as my hard work was. And while I was working like it depended on me, things were happening on the other side that can only be described as God moving. It was like God was saying, "Let me show you *My* way to handle this situation."

Ivy and I have always been "givers." If we have any extra money, we are always looking for people to bless. This time, it was people giving to us. We hadn't said much publicly about our situation or asked anyone for money. Very few people were privy to knowing how serious our circumstance truly was. We were fully content with putting our heads down and working hard to come up with all of that money on our own.

When news of our predicament started to spread about how we lost our house but insurance was denying coverage, people started to bless us. Money was coming from people we had helped in the past. It was coming from people we barely knew. It was coming from old sponsors from my bull riding days and friends from my childhood. Unmarked envelopes of cash were sitting in our mailbox. I was blown away and didn't even know how to react. In one instance, a family sent us a $10,000 check. When I called to thank them, they were shocked to learn about the situation with our house. They aren't on social media and hadn't heard anything about it. Their reply was, "While praying that morning, we felt God leading us to send you that money, so we were simply being obedient." God was showing me that *His* options are far greater than what I thought was the *only* path to a new home for my family.

Three months after the storm, through our business and money given to us, we had already paid off enough of the house to have only $33,130 left on the loan. That number is very specific for a reason.

A FEMA inspector's GPS mistakenly took her six miles out of the way to our address instead of the one she was supposed to be going to. While I was giving her directions to the location she was trying to find, she looked inside our front door and asked if FEMA had been to our house yet. When I told her I had been denied twice by FEMA, she said, "Oh *lawdy* no! I'm here, let me look anyway." After thoroughly inspecting our house, she opened an account with us. She informed us it would probably be 90 days or more until we heard back from them. The very next day, I got a phone call to come down to a temporary FEMA office in the area.

Most of the people I knew who got assistance from FEMA after Harvey received low-interest loans. I was hoping for the same. While it would be nice to get a grant, I knew it was very rare to get one. A loan must be paid back over time. A grant isn't required to be paid back at all. When I walked into the temporary FEMA office, I was told, based on the report given by the inspector the day before, that I had been approved for a full grant for the *max* amount they were able to give from that office. They apologized that they couldn't give more, as the report emphasized that the house was totaled. I was grateful they were giving us *anything*. They then handed me a check … for $33,130. *Exactly* what we had left to pay off our loan.

You can believe whatever you choose to believe. But, as for me? It is experiencing, living through, and witnessing intricately precise moments like this where it is *impossible* to convince me that there is no God.

We went from what seemed like an inconceivable situation to only three months later being able to completely pay off the loan on our property and home. We didn't want to wait to have a new house built on that property, as the black mold was getting unbearable to live with at this point. So we decided to move to Tarkington, closer to the school where my wife was a 5th-grade science teacher and where my kids both went to school. We looked at many houses, but everything was either out of our budget or required a lot of fixing-up. We were approved for a loan to buy a cute little country home with some land and a fishing pond a few miles from the schools. But the people selling us the property backed out at the last second when a better offer came in, which meant a couple more months living in our black mold-infested house. At this point, we weren't even rattled by it. Then the perfect dream home came available at an *incredible* price, and they were asking exactly what we had already been approved for on the country home. It was only one block away from the Tarkington schools … so close, you could actually see the window to my wife's classroom from the back yard of this home.

The following week, we made another huge bonus in our business. Between that and some help from my grandparents, we had enough to put a sizable down payment that locked in an even better, very favorable, low-interest loan on a newer, better dream home than what we had lost. We sold the damaged house for $250 to a guy who picked it up for whatever scrap he could salvage. Other close friends were in need of a new home, so we sold them the property for the bare-minimum the state required to transfer it over to their name, passing on the blessing that had been bestowed upon us. They were able to use the extra cash to haul in dirt to build the property up even higher, and put a nice home there as well.

I am reminiscing on this whole story as I'm typing it out and it still doesn't seem real. In that one dark moment, I was convinced there was only one option to help my family. But a short time later, we got our new home and I didn't have to kill myself to get it.

Work like it depends on me. Pray like it depends on God.

Chapter 14

We Don't Deserve Dogs

Nick's dog, Paris, living her best spoiled life

Being a cowboy, at its very essence, is to care for and protect animals. That's the *true* calling of a cowboy. Everything else is just for show. Wearing a cowboy hat or boots isn't what makes someone a cowboy. That just means they have good fashion sense. Owning horses or cows doesn't make them a cowboy, either. That just means they have some really cool pets. The title of "cowboy" is *earned.* And unless someone's heart is completely consumed with doing everything in their power to care for and protect animals, they will never earn that title.

Cowboys see themselves as commissioned by God to protect His creations, and they don't take that task lightly. To kill an animal is to either protect their livestock from a predator, or provide food for their family – or, in the case of a rancher, provide food for other families across the country as well. Until then, those animals are that cowboy's responsibility through and through. There is no room for the senseless killing of an animal in a cowboy's code. If a deer is shot or a fish is caught, their meat is never wasted.

I've witnessed the toughest cowboys turn into the most caring, compassionate people when tending the animals they've been entrusted to protect. They will face down a blizzard, putting their own life on the line, until they know that every cow, calf, horse, or colt in their stewardship is safely sheltered to ride out the squall. They put out feed for more than just their livestock during a catastrophic storm. They chop frozen streams with an ax to create flowing water throughout their property, giving every animal that calls their ranch home – from deer to raccoon – any and all opportunity to survive. They roll out bails of hay, so that those critters have a place to nest and stay warm.

Anyone who calls themself a cowboy but harms animals isn't a cowboy. They're a blight on the good name of those who are true cowboys. They are "playing house," pretending to be something they're not. In their minds, they're John Wayne while in reality, they're just Pee-Wee Herman wearing a cowhide shirt covered in fringe. You can't be a cowboy and harm animals foolishly. Those two realities don't mesh. A very successful horse trainer once told me, "If someone has to beat a horse senseless to get it to submit, then they aren't as good of a horseman as they think they are."

Are there bad apples who claim to be cowboys? Absolutely. Just like there are bad apples in every profession of life. Critics of the western lifestyle focus on those few bad apples and try to paint all cowboys in that light. What they don't see is the western justice being served outside of the public view. If someone is idiotic enough to not only beat an animal, but post it to social media, the next rodeo that person attends may find them stripped naked, laying in a puddle of mud behind some horse trailer, with rope marks welted into their skin from head to toe. Western culture has a way of punishing those who bring down the entire industry with their stupidity.

Rodeo is constantly under attack by those who – while their intentions may be virtuous in their own mind – are extremely ignorant of the actual facts of the situation. What they are saying *sounds* good, but it also proves how little they truly know about not only the western culture, but also an animal's anatomy. Someone saying, "That bull is only bucking because they're making him mad by tying a rope around his testicles," immediately tells me they know absolutely *nothing* about a bull's reproductive composition. It *sounds* plausible at face value – "*There is definitely a rope tied to the back of that bull. His testicles are somewhere in that vicinity. They must be tying it around his testicles. It's the only thing that makes sense.*" While that sounds logical in theory, it couldn't be any farther from reality. The bull's testicles aren't even close to where that rope is tied. I honestly don't even know how one could physically get the rope far enough back between his legs to reach the testicles. If someone tries, I want to be there to watch because they will surely lose an arm in the attempt. If this "rope tied around their testicles to make them buck" fantasy were true, I wonder what a flank strap ties around on a bucking mare to make her buck – or a gelding, since his testicles have already been removed.

Facts versus opinions and reality versus feelings on numerous topics always make for counterproductive arguments in today's world of social media, where everyone has an opinion but few are willing to research, or even believe, the actual facts. Both sides are convinced they are right and neither will give an inch on their stance. When you get down to the truth of the argument, you will find that both sides are usually more wrong than either of them are right.

People would rather argue something that sounds good in theory than believe concrete evidence that proves otherwise. Even when faced with multiple pictures of a bull kicking from behind, showing the flank rope nowhere near the bull's testicles, critics scream "*PHOTOSHOPPED!*" They decline to believe what can be proven with their eyes so they can remain clinging to the delusion that has consumed their misled opinion. I, personally, refuse to argue with people who only want to spew vitriol. Many people who engage these trolls in a comment section, honestly, do more harm than good for the public opinion of rodeo.

Since this is such a hotly debated topic, I will try my best to present the facts for those who are willing to actually learn about the "why"s of rodeo. Bulls and horses have a muscle that runs from their side to their hind legs called a flank muscle. This is where the cut of beef known as a flank steak comes from. When pressure is applied to an animal's flank muscle, it causes a reflexive knee-jerk reaction, similar to when a doctor taps your kneecap with a reflex hammer during your yearly physical. A flank rope is tied around a bucking bull's flank muscles to *aid* them in their kicking motion. When their hind end comes up for the kicking motion, that knee-jerk reaction is triggered, aiding them through the kick.

A flank rope, made with soft cotton, does not harm the bull in any way, shape, or form. Nor does it "make the bull buck." Much like a racehorse is bred to run fast, bucking is deeply embedded into a bucking animal's bloodline and DNA. These horses and bulls *love* to buck. When temperatures are cool outside you will actually see them play-bucking around the pasture. A flank rope, or flank strap, is solely there as an aid for the bucking animal.

Think of it like shoes on a basketball player. Could they still play basketball in only their socks? Yes, but they wouldn't be nearly as effective, nor be able to reach their full athletic potential without the grip or extra bounce in their jump that the shoes provide. Their shoes are an aid for that player to better perform at his/her full potential. That's the same concept of what a flank rope or flank strap does for a bucking animal.

I highly encourage everyone to go follow my friends Chad and Jenny Drury over at Nothin' But Try Ranch on social media. They perfectly demonstrate how spoiled these bucking bulls truly are. I've known Chad my whole life, as he and his brother, Shane, were some of the childhood friends who stayed at our house for full summers riding bulls in our arena. If the Drury's bulls are "tortured into bucking," then there is no way any of those bulls would allow Addi, Chad and Jenny's daughter, to climb all over them in the pasture … something she has been doing since she was a little child. On their social media pages, you will watch Addi riding one of their bulls around like a horse in the backpens at a PBR, then watch on live-national television, a few hours later, those same bulls buck off some of the best bull riders in the world.

I cannot emphasize this enough: *Stock contractors do not want to harm their animals.* If anything, these are some of the most pampered animals on the planet. Even though animal welfare is highly regulated throughout every aspect of professional rodeo, stock contractors go above and beyond to protect their livestock regardless of any rules saying they must do so. They have invested *generations* of tightly protected bloodlines into their herds. These horses and bulls are just as much a part of their family as their own kids or grandkids. When a bucking horse or bull dies on a ranch, it brings far more emotion to that stock contractor's family than most families face when their pet dog dies.

No longer living on the ranch has not quelled my cowboy instincts or desires to protect animals. If I wasn't allergic to so many different types of animals, I probably would have pursued a career as a veterinarian. My wife and I rode out Hurricane Beryl trying to protect a baby bird that had been separated from its mother and was being tossed around our back yard by hurricane winds so strong they buckled our area's cell phone tower. After the storm, we were able to reunite the fragile creature with its mother, who was flying yard to yard chirping in search of her baby.

I've always had a soft spot for animals. Honestly, I love animals more than I do most humans. So when my son was begging me to let him get a new puppy, it was hard for me to say "no." I did turn down his request for a while, though. Mainly because we had just lost our beautiful Australian Shepherd, Nina, and I saw how much her death devastated my wife. But we all know the repeated timeline of fatherhood at its essence. "Kids ask for a puppy – dad declines puppy request – kids beg *more* for a puppy – dad declines again – kids recruit *mom* to help beg for a puppy – dad keeps declining but eventually gives in – kids get a puppy – puppy attaches to dad – dad attaches to puppy – puppy becomes dad's dog." That's pretty much how we ended up with Paris, who has turned out to be more of a God-send than a pet.

Her breed is Catahoula. She has beautiful brown brindle stripes on her back and a bright white belly scattered with light brown leopard-patch undertones. I was immediately drawn to her because her colors made her look like a bucking bull. She even came from a ranch that raises bucking bulls: the Hilton Bull Co. Ranch. Since Josh and Keshia Hilton gave us the pup, her only logical name was Paris … Paris Hilton.

While she was "my son's dog," that puppy never left my side from the first moment I held her. She would watch my every move and wait for me to sit so she could lay at my feet or on my lap. I became just as attached to that dog as she was to me. That is why, after two years of owning her, I was heartbroken at the thought of having to give her away. She kept making me pass out – or so we thought. I would be feeling fine. Then Paris would run up at me and start jumping, trying to lick my face. In my attempts to back away, I would crash to the ground, passing out. We were facing the reality that if she kept this up, we had no other choice than to find her a new home.

Then one day, I was in the kitchen and she ran at me from across the room, jumping up like she had so many times before. Instead of suddenly jerking away in reaction, I decided to try something new. I sat down on the tile and leaned my back against the refrigerator. Pretty soon, I woke up from passing out yet again. Instead of crashing to the ground like usual, I was already sitting down and my upper body fell to the left as I passed out. When I awoke, Paris was on my left side, leaning her entire body-weight against me, holding my torso up against hers to prevent me from falling the rest of the way to the ground. That's when we realized that she wasn't *making* me pass out. She was *trying to warn me*!

Through her constant need to watch me, she eventually figured out signs, unseen to the human eye and unnoticed by me, telling her I was getting close to passing out. She was trying to warn me before she had to watch me painfully fall from a standing position yet again. This isn't something new. Some dogs go through rigorous training for this very thing. What is so unique in this situation, though, is that she taught herself this skill all on her own!

Most of me thinks she taught this to herself solely out of love for her master. But there's a small part of me that realizes she desperately wanted to be an "inside dog." She's smart enough to piece together that being utilized as an aid to warn me of a potentially painful crash would mean she would never have to sleep outside another night in her life, as she would be needed by my side to watch me. If those were her intuitions, they were correct. That dog rarely leaves my side when I am home.

If I am sitting on the couch and she sees me potentially having an issue, she will jump onto the couch, trap my body between her and the back cushion, then lay her head across my neck to protect me. If I have an issue that causes me to pass out onto the floor, into a chair, or onto the couch, she will lay on top of me and lick my face until I wake up. I have to admit, though, that this gets a tad annoying whenever she confuses an afternoon dad-nap as me having another passing-out episode. I have started having seizures the past few years. If she senses one coming on, she will crawl under my head and use her body as a pillow to prevent my head from bouncing off the floor repeatedly as my entire body shakes out of control.

As intuitive as she is towards my issues, our other dog is equally imperceptive. I don't blame him, though, as he has his own battle to fight. He's a Miniature Australian Shepherd who is 100% deaf in both ears after being born with what is called cochleosaccular deafness, or white-head deafness. As the American Kennel Club explains, the pigment cells that produce color in a dog's hair produce the same cells essential in developing a dog's ability to hear.[1] So the lack of those pigment cells around the ears at birth not only produced a white head, but also resulted in him being born deaf.

We got him two years after getting Paris. Our friends gave him to my wife when he was still a puppy. He had been sold to a family who returned him when his deafness was discovered. My wife, who is obsessed with her coffee and lattes, named him Otto since his white head with black, white, and brown body reminded her of a foamy macchiato. Over the years he has also been given the nickname "Bubs." In truth, it doesn't matter what we call him. He can't hear it.

We have developed our own version of sign-language to communicate with Otto, which is essential knowledge to

---

1. Maharaj, Nandini. "Deafness in Dogs: Signs, Symptoms, and Treatment." *American Kennel Club*, 24 Apr. 2024, www.akc.org/expert-advice/health/deafness-in-dogs/.

know for what is to come in Chapter 17. "Sit," "stay," "lay down," "go outside," "kennel-up," "are you okay," and each of our names are just a few of the hand-signal commands we have invented. My wife is Italian, and Italians can get a little eccentric with their hand motions while talking. I joke that half of my concussions are from standing too close to her while she's telling a story. It's even funnier to watch the deaf dog whenever Ivy is telling someone a story, because he starts sitting down, laying down, and rolling over the entire story, trying to figure out what she is telling him to do.

One weekend, when he was still a puppy, I was home alone with him. I made a tall, multi-layer turkey, ham, and Swiss cheese sandwich for lunch that would have made Joey Tribbiani proud. I wanted to watch a show while I ate, so I set my plate with the sandwich on a TV-stand in front of my chair. I left it there as I walked into the garage to grab a bottle of water. When I stepped around the corner, back out of the garage, I saw Otto standing on my chair sniffing my sandwich. I hollered "No! Stop!" – out of habit because we all know he couldn't hear me – and took off running toward the living room to stop him. That spike in heart rate caused me to pass out and my forward momentum bounced me across the tile floor of the kitchen and halfway onto the carpet of the living room.

When I woke up on the floor, the puppy had knocked the sandwich off of the plate, and was eating it less than two feet from my face. I came-to in time to witness him enjoy the last two bites of my delicious sandwich. But the agony didn't end there. Not only did I have bruises on my body from bouncing off of the tile floor. Not only did I have a rug-burn across the left side of my face from sliding across the carpet. Not only did I lose my appetite thanks to the nausea that accompanied the headache I got from striking my head on the floor, in what was probably another concussion. None of those were the worst of it. We also found out that Otto's stomach can't handle mayonnaise, which he got plenty of from my sandwich. This was the gift that kept on giving, as that little pipsqueak now had explosive diarrhea over the next two days.

I can't blame Bubs though. His innocent naiveness is what makes us love him even more. Sometimes I think he's faking it and is just playing us with a long-con. Like when he was chewing on a bone one day and I jokingly said, "Can you chew that bone any louder?" Thirty seconds later, he jumped up onto the back of the couch, laid right behind my head, and was now chewing that bone less than an inch from my ear, proving he could, indeed, chew it louder.

I have been knocked out by Otto at least four times because he got too playful and jumped into the side of my head. One time, I was passed out on the floor with Paris standing over me licking my face to wake me up, and Otto was trying to jump up behind her, yielding to his innermost male instincts. Like seriously, dude! Read the room.

In contrast to his lack of awareness, Paris is always hyper-aware of everything I am doing. Even if she is playing tug-of-war with a stuffed-duck toy, sniffing the trail of a squirrel outside, or laying on someone else's lap on a couch across the room, she always keeps an eye peeled to where I am and how I am feeling. This cognizance would end up saving my life. Even to this day, I am blown away by what happened that afternoon.

I usually arrived home a couple of hours before my wife and kids. Our new house came with an in-ground pool. I knew how much my family enjoyed utilizing the pool after school let out on Fridays, so I decided to go outside and clean the pool filters and skimmer baskets before they got home. The heat was just starting to get to me, but I wanted to empty out the last basket to finish this chore. I looked over at Paris to see if I was okay, as she would usually give me a sign if something was about to happen. I tried calling her over to me to check, but I was too close to the pool. She accidentally fell into it one time and it scared her so much that after that day, she never stepped close to the pool for fear of falling in again. Besides, she was focused on a gecko that was taunting her from the side of the house.

I was on my knees and bent over to pull the basket out of the skimmer area on the deepest end of the pool. I felt myself tipping forward as I began passing out. I tried to make a last ditch effort to throw my body backwards before everything went black, but my momentum was already committed forward. The last sound I remember hearing was Paris' feet bounding across the turf as she raced towards me. I passed out, face-first, falling into the deep end of the pool.

When I awoke, I was belly down in the water, but my eyes were above water. It took me a second to realize what was happening. Paris had dove in after me, and was swimming underneath my chin, trying desperately to hold my nose above water. Survival instincts immediately kicked-in and I tried swimming on my own. I don't know how long Paris was holding my head up, but I know it was long enough that she was completely drained of energy. As soon as she knew I was aware again, she stopped swimming. I locked eyes with her as she surrendered herself to her exhaustion, laid motionless on her side, and sank towards the bottom of the pool. She was sacrificing her life for mine.

I wasn't going to let that happen. Even though I'm not a good swimmer myself, I couldn't watch this dog die after what she had just done for me. I dove down and scooped her up over my shoulder. Between her weight and my lack of swimming skills, I couldn't get both of us back to the surface. I let us sink to the bottom and used the floor of the pool to push off towards the side we were closest to. I had to do this twice before reaching the side. On the third push, I was finally able to get both of our heads above water and one arm over the side of the pool to hold our weight up. At this point, we were both exhausted with lungs full of water.

I didn't have enough strength left to lift her out of the pool, so I slowly pulled us around the side with one arm, while holding her limp body over my shoulder with the other. The sound of her coughing up water let me know she was still alive. I was so exhausted and struggling to keep her head above water that I even thought, "Neither of us are getting out of this pool alive." About that time, I got a second wind of strength and was able to push through the pain. When we got to the shallow end, I was able to walk up to the tanning ledge portion of the pool, which was less than two feet deep, and lift her out of the pool. I collapsed onto the deck beside her, spent. I don't know how long we both laid there, but it was a while. We were both breathing heavily, periodically puking up water, with no energy to move, but we were both alive.

That night we planned to grill buffalo steaks from bison off my grandparents' ranch for dinner. You better believe I grilled Paris her own buffalo steak that night. I've always had a tendency to spoil my dogs. But none have ever been, and never will be, as spoiled as this dog has been since that day. I now have a connection with Paris I've never had with any other animal. I know the day will eventually come when we have to say goodbye, as dogs rarely outlast their owners, and I already dread how hard that day will hit me.

Until then, she will live the life of a queen … or hotel heiress. Paris earned a special place in my heart that day, that will forever be reserved for her. It really is true: We don't deserve dogs.

Chapter 15

Learning My Limits

Nick (40) performing stand-up comedy in front of a sold-out crowd at The Texan Theatre

I'm hyper-competitive...always have been. This worked as an advantage back in my bull riding days. If someone told me they whole-heartedly believed I couldn't ride a bull I had drawn ... game on. That always lit a different fire under me that brought out my most competitive side.

I remember when I was still in high school, a professional stock contractor brought some of his younger bulls to a high school rodeo. When I asked him about the bull I had drawn he said, "It doesn't matter. This is my best young bull. You ain't gonna last two jumps." I knew right then I was going to break the golden rule of stock contractor relations: don't spur their young bulls.

You don't want to spur young bulls because you want them to gain confidence just as much as the rider. Usually, this is handled in the practice pen, where a rider can ride the young bull for four or five seconds and then jump off. Hauling that young bull to a rodeo – where entry fees have been paid to compete – creates a murkiness as to if that unwritten rule should be followed. Still, most riders respect it and won't spur a young bull to maintain an amiable relationship with the man hauling bulls they will be riding – especially if that contractor has a pro card.

Most stock contractors loved me getting on their bulls. One reason was because I didn't jack around in the chutes. I was in, ready, and out. My goal was to get ready quick enough that I could nod my head before the announcer finished saying my name. I was probably one of the few riders in history the chute boss always had to tell to slow down, rather than the usual, "*Stop jacking around in there! He ain't gonna stand any better than that! Just nod your head and get with it!*"

The other reason stock contractors loved me getting on their bulls was because I was always overly respectful of their animals. I would sit on them in the chutes early and just talk to them, pet their necks, scratch their back. It was rare to have a bull jumping around, fighting the chutes with me, because we had established a mutual calmness before the excitement of the ensuing battle commenced. Many stock contractors sent their young bulls to my house for us to develop and practice on because they knew they could trust their bulls with me and my dad.

That trust was shattered with this particular contractor. But a challenge had been offered, and my competitiveness wanted to prove a point. That little bull bailed out of the chute, really bucky, and cranked it back to the left immediately. He was too close to the chutes, so instead of completing the spin, he jumped backwards away from the chutes, and that's when I pulled my foot. I wide-gap spurred him, bringing my foot back down to his side as hard as I could, making sure the stock contractor – standing on the back of the chutes only a few feet away – could hear the "thump." Unfortunately, as my foot made contact, I also heard and felt the bull let out a grunt of air. I was *immediately* overcome with guilt as the bull took off running, kicking at his belly, rather than bucking. And, boy, was that stock contractor *mad*. Considering that bull wasn't very rank since that day, he held that grudge for a long time, too.

Seventeen years later – *seventeen!* – I realized he still held that grudge, even if more jokingly than seriously. I hadn't seen him in over a dozen years. I was in Vegas helping my brother with his NFR sale, and this stock contractor was on the committee for the event that year. We caught up with a lot of great conversation, and honestly, I figured he had forgotten all about it. After the event concluded, one of the restaurants at the South Point made up some sandwiches for everyone who worked the event. This stock contractor grabbed a bunch of them for us and started handing the sandwiches out. When he got to me, I extended my hand for a sandwich, saying, "Thank you." He just looked at me, smiled, and said, "You don't get one. You ruined my best young bull." Then he winked at me, so I thought he was joking. It wasn't until he had finished handing out all of the sandwiches that I realized, "Oh! He's serious." So I hopped the escalator down to the casino floor and grabbed me a burger at the Steak 'n Shake.

I'm sitting here thinking through the four or five times someone truly challenged me that I wasn't going to ride a certain bull, and the only time I can recollect bucking off was my freshman year in college. It was the short round, which meant the best bulls from the pen were in the draw. The stock contractor was convinced I was going to buck off his bull that hadn't been ridden yet, and my college roommate was convinced his comments telling me so triggered the switch in my mind where I wasn't going to buck off. My roommate made a bet with him that if I bucked off, my roommate would run through the arena in only his underwear. "But if he *rides* him … *you* have to run through the arena in your underwear." Listening to this conversation unfold, and seeing their handshake seal the bet, added a little extra pressure to the situation. I had watched this bull buck off both of his riders – rather quickly – at the NFR only a few months earlier. I knew it was going to be a challenge, but I couldn't let my roommate down for having that level of confidence in me. It was one of the best bull rides I ever made, until it wasn't. I lost my rope and bucked off at 7.8 seconds. My roommate told me later that, being a man of his word, he was ripping his shirt off while jumping over the back of the chutes to fulfill his debt. The stock contractor put his hand to my roommate's chest, shook his head, and said, "We both won that bet." The handshake from that stock contractor afterwards, telling me I had earned his respect, was a great feeling for an eighteen-year-old kid still trying to make a name for himself.

While my ultra-competitive spirit aided me in my bull riding days, it had the exact opposite effect in my post-concussion days. As my cognitive issues became worse, it was becoming increasingly harder to handle my reactions to losing; even at a simple board game. I would get overly mad and didn't know why. I could still control my emotions enough so that others around me wouldn't notice my anger. Then one night scared me so bad that I realized I needed to make some drastic changes in my life to adapt to my new reality.

We were at a bachelor party for one of my really good friends and had rented a go-kart track for ourselves for the whole evening. It was a smaller round track that replicated a short-track race, and the workers covered the corners with baby powder to make it slick enough to replicate a dirt-track. My experience from dirt track racing gave me a pretty big advantage over the other men, and my competitive nature wanted to use that advantage to whoop them every time I raced.

The night was full of heat races, B-Main races, and a final A-Main race, just like a night at the dirt track. I enjoyed lapping the field during the earlier races, but that put a target on my back. My friends wanted to see anyone but me win the final A-Main race. When my kart got anywhere near a friend's kart in the final 50-lap race, they just turned into me and wrecked me. This was hilarious when my friends were spinning me out … it became a game of passing them without giving them a good opportunity to spin me. But when others … guys who hadn't built that friendship equity up with me … joined in on wrecking me, it went from fun to increasingly annoying. Also, my friends knew enough about my brain injury to know they could push it to a point, but not take it too far and hit my kart too hard. It eventually stopped being funny and my anger was starting to build. My friends saw this and backed off. Another guy, who was having too much fun joining in on hitting my kart any chance he saw, didn't get that memo.

He spun me on a straightaway and my kart stalled-out, sitting sideways on the track. Everyone else turned their karts to avoid me while I tried to get it rolling again. When the same guy who had spun me was rounding the corner on the far side of the straightaway for another lap, I could see he had already made up his mind he was going to smoke my kart again. It was like slow motion – reliving my dirt track crash from years earlier where a car came out of the dust and t-boned me – as I watched him heading straight for me. Sure enough, he slammed into my left side, and everything went black.

My next memory was sitting in the driver's side of someone's truck. My friend, Stephen, stood in the open doorway beside me, trapping me in. I thought I'd been knocked out, but apparently I hadn't. Something even scarier happened. I blacked out, and although I was physically conscious, I don't remember anything that happened over the next ten or so minutes. According to them, I bailed out of my kart and hunted that guy for a fight. I was going to rip his head off of his shoulders with his helmet still attached, and any part of his face that didn't tear off with the chin strap I was going to pound with my fists until it became fused to his tailbone. Stephen and another guy cut me off before I could reach him. Even though both men are bigger than me, I was still trying to split between them to reach my destination of fist to face. They had to pick me up and carry me, still swinging, into the parking lot and sat me in the driver's side of the nearest truck. When my blood cooled, I finally came out of my angry trance and back to reality.

The fact that I could glaze over that much was extremely alarming to me. I realized that my shortened fuse could now get to a point where I wouldn't be cognizant enough to control my emotions. I knew I had to make changes. As much as I liked competition, the embarrassment from that night was enough for me to take a hard step back from doing anything that would draw out the highly competitive side of me. I won't even play a board or card game anymore unless I know my mind is in the calmest of places before we start.

That would become my new reality: learning to adapt to what I could and couldn't do anymore. As more issues arose from my concussions, I had to cut more enjoyable things from my life.

Playing golf was my first hobby to go. When I started passing out frequently from bending over, it became almost impossible to play a game that involves reaching down to your ball fifty or more times in one round of play. That was the first really hard pill to swallow. I loved golf and had been playing it for years. I would play on my off days while out rodeoing. My dad and I played almost daily when I was home. We didn't have a golf course within sixty miles of us, but we would hit golf balls at hay bales out into the pasture any chance we got. We stored the balls in an empty metal Folgers coffee can we kept by the shop door. We had a border collie-blue heeler cross dog who would watch us hit every ball and remember where every single one landed. Then, throughout the day, she would gather each ball one by one and put them back into the Folgers can until it slowly filled back up. When it was full, my dad and I would hit the golf balls again. So playing golf was not only extremely fun for me, it was also nostalgic. Having to give that up was hard.

Even harder was when I had to stop working out. I pass out whenever my heart rate rises too quickly, so it became painful to have it keep happening around workout equipment or when out jogging. A guy can only pee on an electric fence so many times before he finally finds another tree to pee behind. At some point, the pain outweighed the reward. The first two years after I stopped working out, I gained over 50 pounds. That was even harder to swallow than the golf thing.

The hardest of them all was giving up fishing. Fishing was my escape, but also filled our freezer with plenty of meat to keep my family fed. I went fishing probably three to five times a week. But as it became harder for my body to handle extreme heat, and with how hot it gets in southeast Texas, I found myself getting confused almost every time I was out on the water. I finally made the decision it was time to cut back on that hobby as well. Plus, after the swimming pool incident, we didn't want me passing out into the water either.

I tried new hobbies. I got into gourmet cooking for a while. But I passed out and almost went face-first into the oven one time, so I've cut back on that hobby as well.

I was still finding myself bull-headedly ignoring doctor's orders to scale back my activities outdoors. You can't tell someone who has spent the majority of their life outside that they have to limit their exposure to the outdoors and expect them to follow it. I had to learn the hard way that doctors actually know what they are talking about, and not listening to mine would lead to the worst outcome I had faced yet with all of my concussion issues.

Chapter 16

The Worst Was Yet to Come

Nick (41) performing stand-up comedy in front of a sold-out crowd at Blase's Hall

Bull rider to preacher to motivational speaker to stand-up comedian. How does someone even make transitions like that? I've gone through all of it personally, and still don't think I could give you a good enough answer for that question. I just want to be wherever God wants me to be, blessing whoever He places in my path. My heart is to bless, encourage, help, and brighten the day of others. Each transition I've made since my career-ending injury fulfills that. I use the word "transition" lightly because, technically, I still do the latter three.

This book may focus on the negatives I've dealt with, but in truth, I've had way more wins than losses in my life. With everything I have faced, it's still crazy for me to think back through all of the "successes" Ivy and I have had.

I got to ride bulls professionally, albeit shortened and through a litany of injuries. An extremely small percentage of people in the history of our planet can say they've done that.

I was a core part of the leadership of a church that grew from a couple hundred people to thousands during our time there. I oversaw almost every single ministry within that church at some point and learned extremely valuable lessons that I still use today.

I was blessed to oversee and lead a youth ministry that grew from around a dozen teenagers to averaging hundreds attending weekly, as well as to lead the more than one hundred adult volunteers who served within that ministry. With that growth came supplying weekly youth ministry to dozens of churches scattered around the rural midwestern United States via DVD, before satellite churches were a thing. We didn't just supply them with sermons, but also transition videos, graphics, and videos to play while teens were arriving that included fully produced MTV-style Christian music video shows. I was also honored to train and manage the leaders of all of those locations while we spearheaded that ministry. The craziest part of the accomplishments within that ministry … *all* of that was done while my wife and I were still in our 20s! We started there when I was only 22 and stepped away when I was 29.

What I'm most proud of is seeing so many teenagers we once led now becoming *extremely* successful as adults. It's one thing to have a lot of teenagers show up on a Wednesday night. It's another thing to use that opportunity to instill usable wisdom that influences every aspect of their future homes, careers, and lives. So many of them have found success as engineers, teachers, lawyers, doctors, dentists, entrepreneurs, firefighters, business owners, and even country music superstars. We truly tried to teach lessons that were applicable to all walks of life. The ones who pursued ministry themself bring me the most pride, for they are making an even bigger impact in the lives of others than I ever did.

I got to race cars for a while. That's just cool.

Through lots of hard work, I watched our MLM business grow to well over ten thousand people on our team. It meant the world to me that I was trusted by the leadership who handed me a microphone, as many times as they did, to train and develop leaders within that company. Even though I took a complete step-back from the business side, my wife and I still take their products daily as they have been revolutionary for many of my brain struggles.

I haven't even mentioned my music life in this book. I've gotten to play and sing on stage and in-studio with many extremely talented, very successful musicians.

I've headlined shows throughout the U.S. as a comedian, as well as perform alongside some of my favorite comedians I listened to fifteen to twenty years before the idea of becoming a comedian was even a thought. Even though my comedy career is still in what would be considered its infancy, I've already been able to mark off one of my "top-five goals" I made myself when I first started: performing at the National Cattlemen's Beef Association World Convention, known as CattleCon. My four remaining high-end goals are performing at the Grand Ole Opry, Red Rocks Amphitheatre, Madison Square Gardens, and The White House – solely for the purpose of fulfilling a lifelong dare of crop-dusting the Oval Office if ever given the chance.

I've spoken in front of crowds of thousands, inspiring them with my story and motivating them with what I've learned throughout it. I've been blessed to speak to future professional athletes, giving first-hand warnings of the consequences of ignoring concussions. I've spoken in small rooms full of influential people from Fortune 500 companies, like ExxonMobil, to the movers and shakers who make everything happen behind the scenes within the Texas music industry.

I truly have lived an *amazing* life. I was once a young kid growing up in the middle of nowhere who had one dream: to be one of the best bull riders in the world. I never would have guessed the wild path my life would take and the many crazy destinations it would stop at along the journey. I believe it's because I refused to give up, despite whatever circumstances I've faced. That, and my internal need to put my absolute best into anything I set my mind to doing. If I faced a road block, I didn't throw my sucker in the dirt and quit. I re-routed my GPS, even if that meant paving a new road through a thick, thorn-infested forest that covered me in cuts and bruises enroute to my destination.

Most of my radical career changes didn't happen because I got tired of doing the other. Most happened completely out of necessity. When I couldn't ride bulls anymore, I transitioned into youth and worship ministry. When the brain injury made it too overwhelming to be able to lead all of the complexities that Crossfire Youth

Ministries of Lone Star Cowboy Church had developed into, I transitioned out of that job into a more executive-type role with a smaller church that has a similar trajectory of growth. I still remain with Dayton Christian Center today, and we are witnessing those same exciting stages of growth developing during this period of my writing this book. Motivational speaking has always been something I've done, but it wasn't until recently that I started intently pursuing the corporate side of keynote speaking. All of these roles have been purposefully targeted to helping *others* grow, whether that be spiritual growth, personal growth, or growth in their leadership skills.

Transitioning into stand-up comedy was a completely different story. That's just *fun* … something for me. When I finally decided to fully commit to being a comedian, I had to choose what type of comedian I wanted to be. While my faith in God is an integral part of who I am, and while I do a lot of comedy shows for churches, I didn't want to be known as a "Christian comedian" per se. I just wanted to be a Christian who does comedy. After all of my years of speaking – and making people laugh while doing so – becoming a stand-up comedian was actually a fairly easy transformation for me.

I already had one of the hardest parts of comedy down: stage presence. While I did the open-mic grind to earn my stripes, it wasn't as essential to me learning *how* to perform from the stage as it is to most comedians starting out. That being said, stand-up comedy is the hardest thing I've ever had to do with a microphone in my hand. Speaking, preaching, singing, announcing, emceeing, hosting, interviewing ... throughout my life I've done just about everything with a microphone from stage as you can. Making people laugh from those vocations is easy, because you can catch the audience off guard with your humor. When the *sole* purpose of standing on stage in front of an audience is to make them laugh, it's a whole new animal. It's like some people will sit back, fold their arms, and say, "Alright, funny boy. *Make* me laugh!" The bar for what is considered "funny" from the stage is raised. A humorous story among friends isn't as funny from the stage. It has to be completely re-written with purpose.

I treat comedy like I did my bull riding. Every time I take a stage is a new learning opportunity. If I'm performing at an open-mic, I treat it like I did the practice pen. Even if I'm working on a new bit or a new angle for an established joke, I always take the microphone and focus on one specific thing. When riding bulls in a practice pen, I focused on something like turning my right foot out more, or keeping my elbow on my free arm up. In comedy, I'll use an open-mic to focus on things like pausing between jokes more, or facial expressions, or breaking eye contact to let a joke simmer, then slowly reengaging eye contact to draw the laugh out. I step away from every stage – open-mic, corporate event, or ticketed show – and reflect on what I can do to get better. I'll film when I can, and go over that recording like I did with film of my bull rides, breaking down every transition and delivery, looking for anything I can improve on.

I don't approach comedy with an attitude that people are there for me. *I'm* there for *them*. It's not about me getting laughs from those in the audience. It's a mindset of me *gifting* laughter to someone in the crowd who has been facing an obstacle of their own. I want to give them a moment of joy as a slight reprieve from whatever they are dealing with outside those comedy club, theatre, or dance hall walls.

Speaking publicly and performing comedy both *fuel* me to work hard every day so that I can bless others. The thought of never being able to do either again scared me. But that's what happened shortly after the entire world shut down due to Covid. When everyone else was emerging from their government-mandated cocoons, I personally faced a new fight that, at the time, didn't seem like it could have any positive outcome. Anything I had faced from my concussion issues prior to this day paled in comparison. I was shocked at how one moment could ultimately affect me so strongly.

Covid was hard enough to face as an entertainer as the entire entertainment industry was put on pause. Thankfully for me, my comedy career was still in an early enough stage that I wasn't fully reliant on comedy or speaking income like many of my friends were. Some of the most popular comedians in America found themselves delivering food through companies like GrubHub, DoorDash, and Uber Eats just to be able to keep their lights on.

That doesn't mean the Covid era wasn't inconvenient for my career, though. I was *just* having my first breakthroughs as a comedian when it all happened. The very night the country shut down was supposed to be my first ever time performing with Christian comedian legend Bob Smiley on stage.

I used the time trapped inside my home to more thoroughly study the art of being a comedian. I downloaded every single special of any comedians I liked and went over everything they did with a fine-tooth comb. I didn't study their jokes, other than the writing style within that joke. I studied their deliveries, their mannerisms, what they did with their hand not holding the microphone, etc.

My wife was living through a whole new craziness on her end. Not only was she a teacher, but she had also agreed to be her campus's "tech liaison" at the beginning of the school year. She received a small stipend with a little added work … mainly helping other teachers set up their computers and other small tech-type needs. It seemed like an easy commitment when she made it. That backfired when Covid forced every teacher to move their classes online. This meant my wife was working five times harder than anyone else because she was now responsible for facilitating and training every teacher on how to accomplish this unprecedented feat. Considering the large number of the veteran teachers who barely even knew how to turn on a computer, she had her work cut out for her. I don't think anyone on my wife's entire campus was happier to return to in-person classes than she was.

As Covid restrictions slowly lifted, and people made their way back into normal life, the entertainment industry started back up again as well. Bob Smiley and I eased back into it with a show at a coffee shop in Palestine, Texas, that proved just how desperate people were for entertainment again. The room was packed to every corner, with people lined up out the doors and gathering outside windows to get a peak inside to listen. The drive home saw me filled with excitement from the dopamine rush the laughter of a packed crowd gave. It rivaled that of the adrenaline rush I had been missing.

Over the next two days, my phone rang off the hook as I booked one show after another. My calendar was filling up, and for the first time in my comedy career, I was finally reaping the rewards of the hard work I had put in beforehand. After booking a swing of shows through my old stomping grounds of South Dakota and Nebraska, I needed to find something to absorb my excited energy. I decided I would grab our push mower and cut the acre of grass in our back yard.

Doctor's orders were to limit exerting myself while in the sun, but I had been ignoring that suggestion. What a few tests had found earlier was that some wires had gotten crossed when my brain healed itself from one of my many concussions, and it was causing an adverse reaction to excessive heat. When someone is in extreme cold, their body tries to prevent their vital organs from freezing. To accomplish this, blood is pulled from the extremities and surrounds the core of the body to keep it warm. This lack of blood in the extremities is how people usually get frostbite in their fingers or toes.[1] My brain was triggering this same reaction whenever my body would get excessively hot. Except my brain wasn't just draining the blood from my arms and legs; it was draining blood away from my head as well.

I noticed some effects of this before, but it usually wasn't that big of a reaction. I just got lightheaded, confused, passed out, or threw up. But over the years, it progressively got worse, which caused me to give up some of the hobbies I mentioned in the previous chapter. Even still, I would ignore the doctors and push myself right to the edge every time. I could usually tell whenever I was

---

1. "Cold Stress Facts ." *Office of Environmental Health and Safety*, Princeton University, ehs.princeton.edu/workplace-construction/occupational-health/heat-cold-stress/cold-stress-facts. Accessed 6 Aug. 2025.

having this reaction because my arms and legs would go numb, and I could physically feel the blood draining from my face. Still, I pushed through those warning signs until I passed out. I eventually learned to stop myself short of passing out. Falling to the ground hurts a lot more at forty years old than it did at twenty-five.

This particular day was very hot and muggy … hotter than normal, which is saying something for southeast Texas. I don't know if it was my excitement or just straight bull-headedness, but when I first felt my arms and face getting numb from the blood draining away from those areas, I tried to keep going. I was three-quarters of the way done with the yard and determined to finish it. When I only had a few passes with the lawnmower remaining, I could tell something was definitely wrong … and different than any time before. I had ignored the symptoms for too long.

I collapsed to the ground, letting go of the lawnmower on my way down. I didn't pass out, but I fell because my legs decided to stop working. All four of my limbs weren't just numb, but they hurt. It felt like an extreme version of a leg waking up after falling asleep. My vision was becoming extremely blurry. My arms, legs, and head pulsated in extreme pain and my vision "bent" with every beat of my heart. I could feel my heart thumping against my chest. I got to my knees and crawled into the house the best I could.

Once I finally made it inside, I pulled myself into a chair. I was determined to cool off and catch my breath, as it was becoming increasingly harder to breathe. Paris was going ballistic, trying to get in my lap and lick my face to cool me off. I looked at the light switch on the wall, and then it happened. My eyes locked to that light switch, and no matter how hard I tried, I couldn't look away. I couldn't blink. I couldn't move my arms. I couldn't even swallow. My entire body felt like it was shutting down. I couldn't move *anything*.

It almost felt like an out of body experience. I knew everything that was going on, yet I couldn't do anything about it. I could feel drool dripping down my chin and the burning in my eyes as tears ran down my cheeks from not being able to blink. I sat in a nightmare, trapped inside my motionless body, not able to take my eyes off that light switch … for hours.

When my wife and kids eventually got home, they found me still stuck in this state. Paris's barking alerted them that something was wrong as soon as they pulled up the driveway, so my wife was already alarmed. I could hear their voices, but they sounded distant, like I was sunk deep underwater and they were speaking to me from the surface. My wife knelt in front of me in panic. She started shaking me, trying to get me to respond. No matter how hard I tried, I couldn't focus my eyes to her face, as I continued to look deep beyond her. I *knew* everything happening around me, but was unable to break myself away from whatever was holding me prisoner in my own body.

I could hear my wife praying desperately for me to snap out of it. I felt what I can only guess was my son's hand on my shoulder as he was praying over me as well. And then it happened. I could finally move my eyes. I looked at my wife's eyes, although it still took me a while to be able to focus on them. I started to look around, and noticed my entire left arm had shriveled up by my chest, with my hand curled and fingers locked shut. My right arm was locked against my belly, as if it were sitting in an invisible sling.

I could see the tears in my wife's eyes. I told her I was okay, but she didn't respond. I said it again, still nothing. That's when I noticed I was saying it in my head, but no words nor sounds were coming out. For the first time in my life, and no matter how hard I tried … I couldn't speak.

Chapter 17

Thriving in the Face of Adversity

Nick (42) keynote speaking at the 2025 Biozyme Inc. Dealer Retreat in St. Joseph, Missouri

I don't think anyone who knows me would say that being around me means enduring a lack of conversation. I like to chat. That's no secret.

I can't stand the sound of silence. When I was a kid, if it was too silent around me, then I would snap my fingers next to my ears just to make noise. With the constant sound of ringing in my head that concussions have caused, silence becomes even more insufferable. Hearing only ringing becomes like that medieval torture device that slowly dripped water onto a prisoner's forehead, progressively grinding away at my sanity. If I'm riding in a vehicle, then the hum of the car's tires on the road contrasts against the ringing in my ears, which only amplifies my exasperation. I will combat that "silence" by trying to strike up a conversation with those around me. I'm sure my desire for conversation is equally as irritating to many friends, as most cowboys are fully content with hearing nothing but the thoughts in their minds.

That being said, to be faced with the reality of not being able to speak or make a noise of any kind was petrifying for me.

So what actually happened?

Consistent blood flow to the head is crucial in that it carries much-needed oxygen and nutrients to the brain. During any other instances, whenever I got hot and blood drained from my head, at some point, blood would suddenly rush back to the head in a panic. In many situations, this is what causes me to pass out. For a reason we still don't know, during this particular instance, the blood continued draining from my head and never rushed back in. The prolonged lack of oxygen flowing to my brain caused what is called an Adult Hypoxic-Ischemic Encephalopathy.

CubaHeal explains it way better than I can:

"Adult Hypoxic-Ischemic Encephalopathy (HIE) is a critical neurological condition that may lead to potential permanent brain damage and long-term functional impairments. The brain relies on a continuous supply of oxygen and nutrients delivered through the bloodstream, and any significant disruption can lead to irreversible neuronal injury. The extent of this damage depends on several factors, including the duration of oxygen deprivation, the specific brain regions affected, and the individual's overall health prior to the event.

While HIE is more commonly discussed in the context of newborns, adults who experience a sudden interruption in oxygen and blood flow to the brain may suffer from mild to severe neurological consequences. The degree of impairment varies widely – some individuals may experience temporary cognitive dysfunction and gradual recovery, while others may suffer from permanent disabilities requiring long-term care and rehabilitation.

The effects of HIE extend beyond physical and cognitive impairments, often impacting an individual's emotional well-being, mental health, and social interactions. Many patients struggle with emotional instability following a hypoxic event, as the brain's ability to regulate emotions and cognitive functions may be altered. The long-term consequences of HIE can also lead to social withdrawal, reduced independence, and challenges in performing daily activities, making rehabilitation and psychological support essential components of recovery.

Recovery from HIE depends largely on the speed of medical intervention and the intensity of rehabilitation efforts. Comprehensive rehabilitation programs – including physical therapy, occupational therapy, and cognitive therapy – aim to retrain the brain and body, helping patients regain lost abilities and adapt to new challenges. While some individuals may make significant strides in their recovery, others may require lifelong support and assistive technologies to improve their quality of life.[1]

Although an HIE is technically different from a stroke, it acts very similarly to one. It's honestly easier for me to just say "stroke" whenever explaining to someone what happened, because most people can relate to a stroke and I don't have to spend the next fifteen minutes trying to explain how an HIE and stroke are different.

---

1. "Adult Hypoxic-Ischemic Encephalopathy (HIE)." *CubaHeal*, 26 June 2025, cubaheal.com/adult-hypoxic-ischemic-encephalopathy-hie/.

I wasn't just having an HIE, though. I was having a catatonic-like syndrome reaction to it. According to a study done by ScienceDirect, catatonic-like syndromes can occur after an HIE and manifest as decreased verbal fluency, fixed gaze, organic mutism, and fixed posture.[2] Everything I was fighting fell under this umbrella: my eyes locking onto the light switch, not being able to move, and especially not being able to speak or make a noise.

At this point in our lives, no health insurance company would touch me, which only amplified how hard the road ahead would be. Years earlier, a friend put us in contact with a private health insurance company whose motto was "We don't turn anyone away." They called me just to tell me that after reading through my health history and looking over the medical documents surrounding my brain injury, they were being forced to change their motto; they couldn't afford the risk of me having an even more serious situation. Thankfully, I have a neurologist who has become so intrigued with my ability to still function at a high level, despite the extensive damage to my brain, that he donates his time to me whenever he can, mainly out of curiosity.

My daughter is heading to Texas A&M in a few weeks to begin her journey towards getting her PhD as a neurolo-

---

2. Kim, Katherine, et al. "Successful Use of Electroconvulsive Therapy for Catatonia After Hypoxic-Ischemic Brain Injury." *Journal of the Academy of Consultation-Liaison Psychiatry*, Elsevier, 11 Jan. 2021, www.-sciencedirect.com/science/article/pii/S0033318220302437.

I'm hoping to one day be her pro bono patient. But until then, no insurance meant not being able to stay at a rehabilitation facility. I didn't want to make *any* of what I was dealing with public because I didn't want anyone to feel like they had to help us pay the extremely expensive price tag that accompanies intensive neurological rehab. People had already done more than enough to help us after Hurricane Harvey, and I didn't want to feel reliant on others again. Any rehabbing I had to do would be on my own, with my wife and kids as support.

So there I was, faced with yet *another* career-changing obstacle. Not being able to speak wipes out *everything* I was doing for a living: stand-up comedy, motivational speaking, and even working at the church. I would argue this was potentially my biggest career-changing hurdle I had ever faced ... and I've had some doozies. To be honest with you, I didn't have that kind of fight left in me. I was too tired to learn a new career that would facilitate my new obstacle. I decided that if I was going to work that hard at learning something new, I might as well put that effort into getting my voice back.

My fifteen minutes were up. Time to get to work.

Every single obstacle I had faced in my life before had prepared me for this moment. Every adversity had stripped away the muscle to grow back stronger in preparation for the fight that lay ahead.

If all I can do is repetitive rehab, then I would rehab my brain from the moment I woke up until the moment I went to sleep. I researched every possible rehabilitation method I could find on rewiring the brain for speech. Then I rotated those over and over again, all day long, day after day after day.

I was able to nod or shake my head to answer questions, but that was about the extent of my communication. The words inside my head were clear and without hesitation. But the signal from my mind to my voice felt completely disconnected. No matter how hard I tried to translate my thoughts into words, no noise would come out of my mouth.

Even though my hands stayed locked in a curled position – which came with a constant pain of cramping in my forearms – I could use my arms to do a version of our sign language signals that we made up for the deaf dog if I needed to ask for something. I couldn't write on a white erase board to communicate, as trying to write had the same mental block as trying to speak. No matter how hard I tried, I couldn't get my hand to draw what my mind was telling it to write. I still struggle with writing five years later. Writing words by hand is one of the most brain-fatiguing exercises I do.

One day, I was walking by our upright grand piano that has been handed down through my wife's family for generations. I thought about how much I missed playing music, and at the thought of playing the piano, my left hand uncurled from the locked position it had been in for days. I reached down and played notes on the piano, which caused my right hand to uncurl as well. Tears rolled down my cheeks as I sat at the piano playing, my first sign of any breakthrough. When I stood up to walk away, both hands slowly curled back into their locked position. I immediately sat back down at the piano, and they both uncurled again.

How it was explained to me is that the area of the brain that had been damaged by the HIE was a different area than the part that is triggered by the creative process of playing music. When my brain switched to the creative music side, it unlocked a path in my brain that seemed blocked by the side fighting against the damage of the HIE. So music became my biggest form of rehab and my new avenue to recovery. I would play the piano with one hand while doing brain exercises on my phone with the other hand.

Work like it depends on me. Pray like it depends on God.

I played my guitar until my fingers bled. I would play worship songs I knew and attempt to sing them, but no noise would come out. So, I would sing worship in my mind while my hands played the chords. Soon, I was finally able to make a sound out of my throat. I couldn't form words, but I could make a muted sound. That was a start. That was hope – a hope that kept fueling my faith.

I kept singing my calf-bellowing version of the songs until I could form actual words with my lips. My tongue wouldn't cooperate, but I could get the core shape of the words out. So, that became my new anthem I would sing. I slowed the tempo of the songs tremendously, trying to force myself to articulate the words, despite my mouth not wanting to cooperate. Eventually, I was able to form full sentences – albeit without being able to fully pronounce the words. It would take every effort in me to fight through stuttering, but it was welcomed progress.

We started to let a very small group of people know something was going on, and even then, we didn't give them many details – only what they *needed* to know. We used Covid to our advantage. It was ordinary during that time for someone to not be seen for weeks at a time. The team of people around me respected my desire to keep what I was dealing with a secret, so they helped facilitate the ruse. I would show up to church on Sunday mornings and stay hidden in the green room. I wore a pocket hoody sweatshirt so I could hide my curled hands in the front pouch of the sweater. When people talked to me, I would smile, fighting through a face still sagging, and nod my head in agreement. I'm sure some of them pieced together that something wasn't right, because it is extremely out of character for me to not take advantage of a good conversation. When church started, I would walk on stage, grab my bass guitar, and play. I was limited in what I could play, but I could play. When worship was over, I would walk off the stage back into the green room, quickly putting my hands back into the pouch of the sweater as they curled back into a locked position. I stayed hidden back there until service was over, then we went home. Church members saw me on stage, so as far as I knew, no one was alarmed or thought anything out of the ordinary had happened.

As weeks went by, I could tell the words in the worship I was singing for rehab were starting to take more shape. My tongue followed suit, and I could finally sound out words individually – albeit with long gaps in between. The harder I rehabbed, the more pronounced my words became until I could finally hold a conversation again.

But I wasn't content to stop there. I wanted to speak so well that people wouldn't notice I had any issues at all. So I kept working at it. I pulled up a dictionary on my phone every morning and read every word across multiple pages out loud, forcing myself to articulate every syllable. Thanks to my intense dedication to rehab, I was back on stage performing comedy a little less than *three months* after the HIE. While I could notice my words still slurred, the common person was oblivious.

I would learn, though, that this hard work wasn't a one-and-done thing. If I take more than two days off from dedicated rehab, my speech slips back to slurring words.

A couple more days without rehabbing leads to constant stuttering, then eventually a full loss of speech ability again. So this has now become a *daily* fight for me. I dedicate between two and four hours of rehab every morning. *Every* morning. If I have to leave my house to go somewhere at seven in the morning, then my alarm is set for 3 A.M.

I treat it like the gym. Slow ramp up, heavy lifting, then a slow ramp down. I rotate whatever exercises I am doing for my early ramp up. That rotation includes doing an hour or two of things like block puzzles, Sudoku, Mahjong, Solitaire, etc. After I ramp up with those, then I read at least one chapter in my Bible, followed by reading at least ten words and their definitions from a dictionary. Then comes the intense part: the Peak App – a phone app designed for improving brain health. I go through every daily exercise the Peak App sets for that day, but I do it as fast and competitively as I can. I then begin my ramp down by doing the NYT Wordle and Strands games, all of the brain teasers on LinkedIn, and finish with a relaxing game like Monopoly Go. I do this every morning. Every. Single. Day.

Because of this, I am able to travel and speak or entertain people with comedy. While I wasn't able to fulfill my original goals in life – a career in rodeo – the path I'm on now somewhat fulfills that gap of disappointment I still feel in my soul. People ask what I miss most about riding bulls. Yes, the adrenaline rush was amazing, and being viewed by a child as a modern-day gladiator never got old. But what I miss the most is the camaraderie between rodeo athletes during the hours traveling together or spent in the locker room, behind the chutes, or in a hotel afterwards. I miss getting to meet new people with every city we visit, or the work I was able to do with the Make-A-Wish Foundation to brighten a family's weekend.

Comedy and inspirational speaking have somewhat given that back to me, but in a smaller way. Yes, they are both considered "lonely" professions, as they are mostly spent traveling solo with many nights in a hotel room by yourself. But when I can tour with another comedian, I travel with people who I not only find personally funny, but also who I enjoy spending time around. I like to surround myself with high-integrity men who treat everyone around them with respect; guys like Bob Smiley, Chad Prather, Mark Paul, and Royce Moore.

Meeting new people wherever I perform or speak, and hearing their stories of how my comedy or speech may have impacted them that night drives me to keep going. Getting to speak at a conference, training, convention, school, etc., makes me feel a piece of the same way I felt when I was traveling on the rodeo circuit. Making even the smallest of differences in someone's life is worth all of the hard work to me.

Would I have loved to fulfill my childhood dream as a professional bull rider? Absolutely! But life threw me a series of curveballs, and I had to learn to adapt. While I may not have gotten to spend my life entertaining crowds with a bull rope in my hand, a microphone has made a semblance of that dream a new reality.

If I have to sacrifice sleep to grind away at rehab so I can be functional enough to speak clearly in front of people, then that's what I'll do. If you see me standing on stage – doing comedy, playing music, or speaking – know it was hours of rehab that morning that made it possible for me to be there.

I work hard every single day because I feel I owe that dedication to God to fulfill whatever purposes He still needs me for.

CHAPTER 18

TAKE CARE OF CONCUSSIONS

Nick (36) speaking at an MLM Convention in Dallas, TX circa 2018

I DON'T TAKE LIGHTLY THAT I SHOULD HAVE DIED ON SO many occasions throughout my life. I've had my fair share of bad wrecks, health issues, and momentary concussion-driven weaknesses that *all* could have easily ended in my death. God is not done with me yet. So, I've made it my purpose to not waste my time while I'm still on this earth, and to use my story to help as many people as I can. If that means exposing myself to ridicule or impugnation to get my story in front of someone who needs to hear it, then I've made my bed in this glass house of a book.

I don't see myself or my circumstances as unique or special. Sure, there are many instances throughout this book that almost seem unreal. The end of my bull riding career, the brain injury, Hurricane Harvey, Paris and the pool, teaching myself to talk again. Every single one of those could be a stand-alone book on adversity. Put all of them together, and it almost seems made-up. But I've lived them, and each one has made a lasting impact on me as a person. Forcing myself to write it all down in one book, honestly shocked me. I have endured so many crazy things throughout my life. It's one thing to know they happened. It's another to put them all together and reflect back on them while writing out the details.

I can honestly say this process has been healing for me in many ways. To relive past events, and face the emotions I let control me during those periods of my life, have served as a caution to me while facing newer roadblocks that have surfaced during the process of this book. My life has been one long rollercoaster of emotions, and continues to be so. As one friend once told me, "If you feel on top of the world, hang on because the world turns over every 24 hours."

I put off writing this book for so many years because I never "felt ready." But there-in lies the problem, right? Someone will never "feel" ready, because being ready is not a *feeling* or an emotion; it's an *action*. I held back because I didn't want to project myself as more than I am. I was fearful of the future ridicule I could face because of my lack of accomplishments in the professional rodeo world. There are so many other bull riders who are more deserving of a book, and who have accomplished far more than I ever did. I truly believe I would have accomplished great things as a bull rider, had I been given the full opportunity. But belief in it happening, and it actually happening, can only be a pipe-dream of retrospect.

There are also people in life who have faced far greater adversity than I have ever faced. There are people pushing through daily struggles that make mine seem minute in comparison. So, that feeling of not wanting to project myself larger than how I feel held me back from writing this book for many years. It wasn't until I fully committed to the writing process that I realized the voice I needed to relay.

I may not be the best example, but I'm an example. I may not be able to help everyone, but I can maybe help one. I'm not a "medical expert." I'm just an old, beat-up cowboy who has a tale to tell. If my story can change one life for the better, then telling my story was worth every word.

There are so many people in this world who deal with the adverse reactions from concussions, but they feel alone. They may feel alone because they pushed everyone around them away or because they don't want to ask for help. They may feel alone because their friends and family feel helpless and don't know *how to* help. Or their friends and family don't even know they *need* help.

My goal is to tackle concussion issues head-on, no pun intended. I want to educate the public on the potential problems concussions can cause, not from a medical background but from the standpoint of someone who has personally encountered many aspects of their side effects. I hope my experiences serve as a warning of the importance of letting your concussions heal before subjecting yourself to the risk of another one.

I'm not against the sports or activities that cause concussions. If you get that idea, then you weren't reading the book closely enough. But I am, undoubtedly, an advocate for preventing concussions, letting concussions heal, and taking them seriously whenever one occurs.

I talked about many of my side effects that seem serious in earlier chapters. I didn't talk about the many side effects I have that may not be serious, but that can be very annoying. Like when I'll be in the shower, shampooing my hair, not quite able to figure out why this shower feels different than other showers. It's not until I go to dry off that I realize I never turned the water on.

Or how about my taste issues? Those can get really annoying. Sometimes my brain will be acting up, and food tastes horrible. It will taste like burning rubber or like the smell of a decomposing animal. This happens so often, and I push through the bad taste to finish my meal so often, that whenever my brain *isn't* acting up, and there *is* a problem with the food, I usually don't notice until it's too late. I can't count how many times I have accidentally put cottage cheese on a burrito instead of sour cream – they really need to stop making those containers look so much alike – and write off the bad taste as my brain acting up, only to realize my mistake when my wife asks me why I put cottage cheese on my burrito. Or that time I was eating cereal and thought it tasted like death. Once again, I thought it was my brain, so I pushed through and ate the cereal. It wasn't until I got to the bottom of the bowl that I realized the chunks in my milk I was eating weren't cereal. They were curdled milk. Neither my stomach nor the toilet enjoyed that mistake for the next few hours.

Whenever it *is* my brain acting up, though, it usually stays that way for a few days. So those are the days I try to eat healthy, because the only thing holding me back from eating healthy is the taste. Usually, I stick to what I call the Osmosis Diet. I let the cow eat my salad. Then I eat her. Now I'm eating healthy by osmosis. Does it work? No. But it sounds good. So, when my brain makes everything taste bad, I chow down on all healthy meals because it already tastes bad anyway. It may not be the soundest logic, but it makes sense to me.

While we may laugh at these instances now, it doesn't diminish the seriousness that stacking concussions on top of each other can bring. If you deal with concussions, please don't ignore them. Don't blow them off as just a minor thing. They may seem like nothing at the time, but they have the potential to be life-altering if you don't let yourself fully heal before returning to the activities that caused them. People have different reactions to concussions. How many concussions it takes before someone pushes over that edge-of-no-return is different for everyone. You may be able to handle them better than others at first. So did I. But they will catch up to you eventually if you let them pile up. How many concussions can someone have before they hit that threshold? I don't think they want to find out. Getting a concussion doesn't mean you are weak. Taking a step back to heal from a head injury doesn't make you weak, either.

Don't let your concussions become a crutch of excuses. Having concussion issues should never be an exemption for taking your anger out on your family or those around you. This is something you *can* control. It will just take more effort than it did before you had any concussions. Simply writing off someone's aggressive behavior as being solely because of concussions is not healthy for that person, nor the people in that person's life.

Don't let your concussions become an anchor tied to your leg that drags you down with it. Is life harder now? It sure has been for me. That should never be a justification to quit trying, though. Don't give in to them. Learn to combat them. Find what works for *you*. Learn your new weaknesses, and adapt to not let those weaknesses control you.

Maybe you're a reader who has never had a concussion. I still hope this book helped you face something else you may be dealing with. Everyone deals with some level of adversity throughout their life. I hope my story can inspire you to push through whatever it is you're facing, have faced, or will face in the future.

Take those fifteen minutes, however long that is for you, but eventually make up your mind to move forward. You can't change the past. It's time to start focusing on the future.

Don't let yourself get bitter at your circumstances or bitter at those around you. Bitterness is dangerous because you're usually the last person to realize you're bitter. It's time to get better, not bitter. You can't be both.

Seize opportunities to learn and improve in every aspect of whatever you put your mind to. Win or lose, every opportunity should be a new opportunity to learn something. You're not a loser until you start acting like one.

Control your mentality, the *attitude* of your mind. Your mindset is a powerful tool. If all you focus on is the negative around you, all your mind will perceive is the negative side of every situation. But if you choose to rewire your mind to focus on the positive, you will see life, and everything around you, in a completely new light. That one purposeful action can be extremely liberating to those who choose to pursue it.

I truly hope you enjoyed this book. I hope it helped you learn something new and insightful. But most importantly, out of everything you have read, if there is anything you have taken away from this book, it should be this:

Take care of concussions.

Rodeo/Cowboy Terminology

Backpens: a rodeo term for the pens holding bucking horses and bucking bulls during a rodeo. They are pens located behind the bucking chutes, hence the name backpens.

Bareback Rider: rodeo athletes who compete in the bareback riding discipline. Not what you thought that meant, huh? Believe me, just the thought of having to explain myself whenever telling someone outside of the rodeo world that "I'm a bareback rider" was enough to make me not pursue this discipline. That being said, these guys are *tough*. I don't believe there is another discipline in rodeo that beats on the body more than bareback riding.

Bareback Riding: a rodeo discipline where the athlete rides a bucking horse with a spurring motion on the horse's neck that goes from above the horse's shoulders, up to the front of the bareback rigging, then back to above the horse's shoulders. The term "bareback" is referring to the fact the cowboy is laying on the horse's bare back, with no saddle, and only a bareback riggin' to hold onto. The rider must stay on for 8-seconds and is then given a score based on the performance of the horse and rider. *To see how a score is calculated, refer to "Score".*

Bareback Rigging: a rodeo term referring to the equipment used for bareback riding, often referred to as a *"riggin'."* It is made of leather and rawhide. The body of the riggin', shaped like an upside-down "v", lays across the horse's back, just behind its withers. It is secured to the horse by a cinch, made of mohair, that runs under the horse's belly, right behind their front legs. The cinch is connected to the rigging by leather straps, called latigos, on each side. On top of the riggin' body is a hard, stiff rawhide handhold that is shaped similar to a suitcase handle. The rider maneuvers his hand into this handle, while leather binds glued to the inside of the rider's glove are essentially wedging their hand in place.

Barrel Horse: horses used for the barrel racing discipline of rodeo.

These are very strong, very fast animals who love what they do. They are also very high-strung and will not hesitate to run over you in a heartbeat.

Barrel Racer: rodeo athletes who compete in the barrel racing discipline of rodeo. We joke that these ladies are "just as crazy as their horses", but the reality is they are great ambassadors for the sport of rodeo and a staple of the rodeo community. Don't ask anyone who works as grounds crew for an arena about barrel racers, though, because I guarantee they are the ones who started the "barrel racers are crazy" stereotype.

Barrel Racing: a rodeo discipline where a female athlete rides their horse around three barrels in a cloverleaf pattern. The pair of horse and rider are timed for how long it takes them to cross the start/finish line, turn around all three barrels, and then cross back over the start/finish line. They are assessed a five-second penalty for every barrel they knock over during their run.

Barrelman: what many people outside of rodeo refer to as the "Rodeo Clown." These men wear many hats and are the backbone of any rodeo event. They entertain the crowd throughout the event with quick jokes and specialty acts. Then, during the bull riding, they are invaluable to the bull riders and bull fighters with the placement of their barrel, which they remain inside of, to be used as a shield from the bull, if needed.

Barrier: a rodeo term referring to a rope stretched across the roping box used during the timed events. It is connected to a "pigtail" by a small string which connects to another rope that extends around the calf or steer's neck. It is designed to give the calf or steer a head start before the horse and rider can leave the box. If the calf or steer hits the end of their rope first, it breaks from around their neck and releases the barrier. If the rider leaves too early, then they will break the string around the pigtail first, indicating they left too soon. This is called "breaking the barrier" and assesses a ten-second penalty to their run.

Belly Roll: a bull riding term for when a bull kicks sideways while bucking, essentially rolling his belly and back to the side. Bulls may use a belly roll technique back and forth, one way then the other way, in an attempt to get the rider's momentum moving from one side to the other.

Bloop Spinner: a rodeo term for a bucking bull that always spins, has a lot of rhythm to his bucking motion, and doesn't throw any tricks at the rider. They are a reliable, fun bull to ride because a rider doesn't have to think much while on them but can just let their instincts ride the bull. Another term for these types of bucking bulls is "spur bait" because a rider will usually spur this kind of bull in an attempt to improve their score.

Breed Bulls/Breeding Bulls: bulls used on a ranch for the sole purpose of breeding.

Bronc Rein: a rodeo term referring to what a saddle bronc rider holds onto during his ride. It is a loosely braided rope, usually made of poly or sisal, attached to a halter on the horse's head. Where you hold onto the rein is crucial to making a qualified ride. Too short of a rein will pull you over the front of the horse. Too long of a rein will make you lose leverage and risk "running out the back of the saddle". Bronc riders use a measuring system to determine where to hang onto the rein, determined by how much a horse lowers or raises their head while they are bucking. While still in the bucking chute the horse's head is held straight, and the rein is pulled snugly over the swells of their saddle. The rider then holds the rein in his fist against the swells, with his thumb extended to determine the average length for that horse, which is considered "X". Based on how much a horse "takes her head" determines if you need to grab lower or higher than X on the rein. This is measured by "width of fingers". So if a stock contractor tells a rider that the horse he has drawn "takes X plus 2" that means the rider will measure two fingers next to his extended thumb, and grab the rein in that spot with his riding hand to hold onto during the ride.

Bronc Riders: *see Saddle Bronc Riders*

Bronc Saddle: *see Saddle Bronc Saddle*

Bucking Bull: bulls bucked in the sport of rodeo. The bloodlines of a bucking bull are much like the importance of bloodlines in racehorses. Bucking is deeply embedded in their blood. They are handled from a young age and pampered their entire life. They are fed the best feeds, given the best supplements, and have the latest advancements in medicine at their call, if needed. They train and prepare, like any professional athlete, for one thing: to buck. Bucking bulls nowadays are even running on treadmills in an alleyway, if you can believe it. Many bucking bulls become superstars to rodeo fans. Their athleticism, despite their massive size, is insane. It's like watching an offensive lineman dodging tacklers like Barry Sanders. How high they can jump. How fast they can move. How hard they can kick. Muscles rippling throughout their entire body. Snorts of confidence…..I need to stop because I'm about to break-out into a Tim Allen gruntfest.

Bucking Chute: where all roughstock rides begin their journey. Bucking bulls and bucking horses are loaded into the chutes through an alleyway before they buck. This is where the ropes, riggins, or saddles are put on, and where the rider climbs on the animal to prepare for the ride. When the rider is ready, he nods his head and a gate on the side of the chute is opened to begin the ride.

Bucking Horse: a horse used in the bareback riding or saddle bronc riding events. These horses are bred to buck, with generations of bucking horses running through their veins. These are very smart, extremely athletic animals. Not only do they know what they are doing at all times, they *love* bucking. Veteran bucking horses will strut around the arena after a good trip with their chest bowed out, soaking in the crowd and the moment. These big-footed muscular braumbies are magnificently beautiful creatures. Much like watching a basketball player in their element on the basketball court, it is equally as satisfying, if not more, to watch a bucking horse living their best life, basking in the limelight of a rodeo arena.

Bucky: a rodeo and cowboy term used to describe a young bull or horse who bucks hard. If it's a bucking horse or bull, bucky is meant as a positive compliment and a sign of a bright future for that animal. "That little guy is pretty bucky."

Buck Off/Bucked Off: a rodeo term referring to when a roughstock rider is thrown from the animal before the 8-second buzzer sounds. A buck off results in a no score.

Building Fence: *see Fixing Fence*

Bull: a male bovine who has not been castrated.

Bull Fighter: studs. I wish I could just leave the definition there, because that's exactly what these men are. They are the protectors of the bull riders. They lay their lives on the line with every bull that bucks. They have one job in mind: to keep the bull rider safe. There are usually two to three bull fighters at an event, and they work together as one. Whenever the best bull fighters in the world are working "the blender", I find myself watching them more than the bull riding. Their positioning and synchrony are a work of art. These guys are heroes in their own right, and as manly as they come. It's how a Ten-Time PRCA Bull Fighter of the Year can be as bald as Danny Devito, yet still be the manliest man in the room……love ya, Tuck.

Bull Rider: rodeo athletes who compete in the bull riding discipline. Just getting on bulls doesn't make a person a bull rider, much like playing backyard football with their family at Thanksgiving doesn't make them a football player. The title of "bull rider" is *earned* the first time they ride a good one for the full 8-seconds. Until then, they're just a bull getter-onner. Bull riders are considered the "gladiators of the sport." Many are also the "skateboarders of the sport." While many bull riders are extremely handy around a ranch, if I was to hear that a rodeo athlete made a fool of himself trying to do "cowboy stuff," I would bet money he was a bull rider.

Bull Riding: a rodeo discipline where the athlete rides a bucking bull. There is no spurring motion required. Since half of the score is based on how much control the rider had, bull riders may choose to spur a bull to prove they are in full control, and influence extra points. A spurring motion in bull riding is made with whichever leg is on the outside of the spinning bull. It constitutes a motion of dragging the foot up the side of the bull, then kicking out and back down. The more space there is between a rider's leg and the bull during a spurring motion, the more influential the spurring motion is over their score. The rider must stay on for eight seconds and is then given a score based on the performance of the bull and rider. *To see how a score is calculated, refer to "Score".*

Bull Riding Event: a rodeo event that only features the bull riding discipline. This is talked about in more detail in Chapter 6.

Bull Rope: a rodeo term referring to what a bull rider hangs onto while they ride. This is not at all like a rope, or lasso, most people picture when they think of a cowboy with a rope. The design of a bull rope has three parts: the tail, the block, and the body. A bull rider uses glycerin and rosin to make approximately a two foot area of the tail sticky. This area is usually blackened by the rosin, which hardens when it is cooled. Friction created by introducing new rosin to the rider's glove, and quickly running it up and down the blackened part of the tail, warms this area and creates a sticky section to wrap around the hand to prevent the tail from slipping through the rider's glove. The block houses the handle. Usually a leather pad is attached to this section of the bull rope that goes between the bull's back and the block. Braided out of the other side of the block is the body, which is tied into an adjustable knot. It is essential for rope-health that this knot be un-done every time the rope is put away, and re-tied every time it is used. The block is placed on the bull's back with the body going under the bull's belly and the tail looping through the body and back up to wrap around the rider's hand in the handle. The knot on the body is adjusted to fit the bull's girth and guarantee the rosined part of the tail is fully in the rider's hand when the rope is pulled tight. The higher the knot is on the rope body (and bigger the loop it creates), the smaller the bull. The lower the knot is on the rope body (and smaller the loop it creates), the bigger the bull.

Buzzer: a rodeo term for an audible noise to let the roughstock contestant know they have made a qualified ride. When the animal leaves the chute, a timer is started once the animal's inside shoulder crosses the plain of the gate. A buzzer then sounds over the PA system 8 seconds later, letting the rider know he has made a qualified ride and can now get off of his animal. This is also referred to as "*the whistle*" since a metal whistle is usually blown by a rodeo secretary or timer in the crow's nest, if a buzzer is not available.

Calf: a young bovine offspring.

Calf Roper: a rodeo athlete who competes in the calf roping discipline. They are the "pretty boys" of the rodeo world with their heavily starched shirts, clean-cut jeans, and pearly white smiles. Imagine a slick New York lawyer wearing western attire, and you've got yourself a calf roper.

Calf Roping: a rodeo discipline where the athlete ropes a calf from their horse, dismounts their horse, then flanks and ties three of the calf's four legs. This discipline mimics what cowboys do to administer medicine to calves on their ranch. The contestant is timed from the moment the calf leaves the roping chute until the contestant throws both hands in the air after tying the calf's legs.

Chaps: protective gear for the legs of athletes competing in the roughstock events. They are made of thick leather and protect the legs when getting kicked or stepped on. Leather fringe goes down the backs of both legs solely for style purposes. Athletes use the chaps to express individual style with differing patterns and colors. Chaps can also be used to display an athlete's sponsors.

Chilly-Whopped: *see Yard-Darted*

Chutes: *see Bucking Chute or Roping Chute*

Chute Boss: a rodeo term for the person in charge of keeping a rodeo running in a timely manner. The chute boss walks back and forth in front of the chutes, telling the riders when they will be competing. "Three to you." "Two to you. Start warming that rope up!"

Circuit Rodeos: a rodeo term for a professional rodeo held at a location within a professional athlete's declared circuit. The PRCA is split into 12 regional circuits. Every PRCA athlete must declare for one of those circuits, regardless of if their home address is within that circuit or not. While many compete at rodeos all across America and Canada, any money won at a rodeo held at a location within their declared circuit counts towards their Circuit Standings. Each circuit has its own Circuit Finals, with both the Year-End Champion – based on total money won – and Circuit Finals Average Champion qualifying to the RAM National Circuit Finals Rodeo currently held in Kissimmee, Florida. It was previously known as the Dodge National Circuit Finals held in Pocatello, Idaho, since its inception in 1987, before moving to Oklahoma in 2011 and eventually Florida in 2015. The Circuit aspect of the

PRCA adds another layer for athletes to compete and win money, while also giving an opportunity to find success professionally for those athletes not wanting to chase a World Title or NFR Qualification by traveling all over the US and Canada year-round. The five most prestigious year-end titles to win in the PRCA are, in order, All-Around World Champion (most total money won by contestants who compete in two or more disciplines), World Champion, NFR Average Champion, NFR Qualifier, and Ram National Circuit Finals Champion.

College Rodeo: the sport of rodeo at the Collegiate level, governed by the NIRA (National Intercollegiate Rodeo Association). Many people outside of rodeo may not realize that not only can you compete in rodeo collegiately, but many colleges around the nation have college rodeo teams complete with coaches, trainers, and practice facilities. Many college rodeo athletes attend school on a rodeo scholarship. What makes rodeo unique to any other sport, to my knowledge, is that you can compete both collegiately *and* professionally at the same time.

Cover/Cover A Bull/Covered My Bull: a rodeo term that is another way of saying the roughstock rider made a qualified 8-second ride.

Cow: female bovines.

Crow's Nest: a rodeo term referring to a structure where the announcer, timers, and secretaries are usually located during the rodeo. It is typically located above the middle of the bucking chutes. The term "crow's nest" is derived from the sailing term used to depict the structure on a ship's mast used as a lookout point.

Dally: a cowboy and rodeo term referring to the act of a cowboy wrapping their rope around the saddle horn after catching an animal. It is common for a roper to get their fingers trapped between the rope and the saddle horn while doing this action. If they don't get their fingers out of the way, their finger(s) are usually cut off. Dallying is a requirement of both the header and the heeler in the team roping discipline. So, if you shake a cowboy's hand and he has multiple fingers shorter than normal, or is missing a thumb, it's a pretty good chance he is a team roper.

Draw/Drew/Drawn: a rodeo term referring to the livestock the contestant is matched against on that day. *"I drew J47 Heart Attack." "I have a good bull drawn in Reno this weekend."* In bull riding, for instance, all of the bulls brought to the event are written down and their names, or brand numbers, are written on poker chips and placed in a hat. The judges for the event then go down the contestant list and physically draw a chip out of the hat, with each contestant's name, to determine what bull that contestant will be riding. The riders will then go "check the draw" posted outside of the secretary's office to see what they are riding that day. At the professional level, this draw is done days before the rodeo so the contestants know, well in advance, what animal they will be riding. While many rodeos still draw physically from a hat, with today's technology, many times this is done by random computer draw as well.

Dropped In The Well: a bull riding term referring to the rider's body dropping inside the spin of a bull. The "well" is considered anywhere inside the spin, while anywhere outside of the spin is simply referred to as "outside." We may not want to admit it, but bull riding has a lot of similarities to ice skating when it comes to force and momentum. When a bull is spinning in one direction, common thought would be that their force is pushing the rider to the outside of that spin. This is definitely the case if the bull's momentum is moving into the spin, aka the same direction as the spin (centrifugal force). But if that bull's momentum is moving *away* from the spin, their force will actually *pull* the rider into the well (centripetal force). Think of it like watching from above as a top spins on a table. If a bull is spinning to the left but drifting to the right, he will actually be "sucking" the rider down into the well. If a bull has a reputation for this action, he is known as being "welly". Smart bulls will switch up moving into and away from the spin, trying to use the rider's momentum, in combating the centrifugal or centripetal force, against them. These bulls are *very* intelligent, and the 8-second ride can become as much a chess-match between the rider and bull as it is a battle of attrition and athleticism.

Fixing Fence: a ranching term for mending barbed wire fences around the ranch. This may constitute actions like digging new post holes, building a new corner, replacing broken wire, building a new gate, or more. "Building fence" requires the same actions, except you are building the fence from scratch rather than simply mending a section of the fence. Working cows horseback may be the Hollywood cowboy dream, but fixing and building fences is the majority reality of being a ranch cowboy.

Flank Rope: a soft cotton rope that wraps around a bull's back and flank muscles. The slight pressure applied to the flank muscle by the soft cotton rope causes a "knee-jerk" reflex reaction that aids the bull in his kicking motion. This rope *is not* tied through or around the bull's testicles, like erroneously reported by misguided activists, to "cause them to buck." I go over this in great detail in Chapter 14.

Flank Strap: a variation to the flank rope that is used on bucking horses. It is made of leather, with the section touching a horse's flank muscles surrounded by thick, soft sheepskin. The difference with a flank strap is that it can be tightened by the stock contractor during the motion of the horse leaving the chute. As with the flank rope, a flank strap does not harm nor hurt the horse in any way, but rather aids the horse in their kicking motion by applying slight pressure against the flank muscle, triggering a "knee-jerk" reflex reaction.

Free Hand/Free Arm: the hand not holding on to a bull rope, bareback rigging, or bronc rein in the roughstock events. This hand may not come into contact with the animal, rider, or any of the rider's equipment during the 8-second duration or else it will result in a no-score.

Gathering (The Herd/Bucking Horses): a ranch term used for gathering livestock from the pasture and herding them into pens, usually back at the ranch headquarters. Gathering bucking horses is one of the most majestic things a person can experience. Riding your saddle horse behind a herd of bucking horses, running up and down hills, with their manes blowing in the wind and the resonating deep sound of their collective hooves across soil will trigger the *Man From Snowy River* soundtrack in your mind almost every time.

Gelding: a male horse that has been castrated. Stallions can be very dangerous and territorial around other stallions, whereas geldings are not. On most ranches, if a stallion is not going to be used for breeding then he is gelded.

Head: a cowboy and rodeo term used to communicate the number of livestock, i.e. "100 head of cattle" or "75 head of horses." This is one of the oldest terms in cowboy vocabulary that is still used today. It derives from the old west days when cattle were being shipped from stockyards in the west to cities in the east via trains. When the cattle were in the alley, before being sold and loaded onto the train cars, cowboys would have to count the cattle. Since all of the animals were in close proximity to each other, usually the heads of the cattle were the easiest thing to see. So, cowboys would count their heads. "*I counted 138 heads. How many did you count?*" And so the term was born. "Head" has since become the universal term when describing the number of livestock. "*I run around 500 head in that pasture*". In rodeo, if it is a three-head event that means you will be competing in three rounds, or riding/roping three animals.

Header: team roper who ropes the head side of the steer.

Heeler: team roper who ropes the feet side of the steer.

Heifer: a young female bovine who hasn't borne a calf yet.

Hop and Skip: a rodeo term referring to a move made by a bucking horse or bull during a roughstock event. A hop and skip is essentially a shortened jumping motion the bull or horse will use to disrupt the timing of the rider.

Hooked On/Hooking: a rodeo and cowboy term for when a bull or cow is hitting a person with their head or horns.

Hung Up: a rodeo term for when a rodeo athlete's hands or feet are caught in their equipment still attached to the animal, while the rider is no longer on the back of that animal. This could be a riding hand in the bull rope for bull riders, a riding hand in the riggin' for bareback riders, or a foot in the bronc saddle stirrup for saddle bronc riders. Saddle bronc riders wear looser fitting boots and fill them with baby powder before each ride, so the boot will come off immediately if they do get hung up. Most bull riding hang ups happen from getting bucked off on the opposite side of your riding hand.

INFR: the Indian National Finals Rodeo, a non-profit rodeo organization that promotes rodeo within the Native American culture. Contestants must be a card-carrying member of a Native American tribe to compete. The INFR is held every year in Las Vegas, Nevada, at the South Point Casino and Resort. Contestants qualify to the Finals through their Tour standings from designated INFR Tour rodeos, winning the season title in their regional circuit standings, and various Last Chance Qualifier events.

In The Latch: a bull riding term for a bull spinning as soon as the gate opens. The gate is held shut by a latch that an arena crew lifts to open the gate when a rider nods his head to start the ride. So the term "he turned back in the latch" means he started spinning immediately, rather than jumping out two or three jumps before spinning. To say a bull is "in the latch to the left" or "in the latch to the right" denotes that he normally spins immediately, and it is telling you which direction he usually spins.

Jerked Down: a bull riding term for when a rider's upper body is quickly pulled down onto a bull's head while the rider is still on the bull's back, or in the process of being bucked off. This is where most concussions occur in bull riding.

Jerked The Rope Out Of My Hand: a bull riding term for when a bull's power jerks the rider's hand out of the handle. A hop and skip move by the bull into a powerful jump can cause this to happen due to the quick movement of the hand against the handle. *See also Lost My Rope*

Judges: a term for those who officiate rodeos. They have many jobs at any single rodeo. Before the rodeo they are responsible for monitoring a fair draw, with many performing the draw themselves. During the roughstock events, one judge standing on the back of the chutes has a stop watch to record the official time to determine if a rider makes a qualified ride or not. The other judges in the arena give a score based on what they see from the side they are standing on. In the timed events, one judge sits on a horse in an arena with a small flag held in their hand. When the contestant has done everything to complete their run, the judge drops their flag in a downward motion, signaling to the timer in the crow's nest to stop the time. The other judges are by the roping chute and roping box maintaining the barrier, and signaling if a contestant broke the barrier or not.

Long Go-Round/Long Go/Long Round: a rodeo term for the round(s), in a multiple round format, that features every entered contestant. Based on how a contestant places in the Long Go will determine if they move on to the Short Round or not.

Lost My Rope: a bull riding term for when your hand comes out of the bull rope's handle while still on the bull's back. *See also Jerked The Rope Out Of My Hand*

Mare: a female horse.

Mark Out Rule/Marked Horse Out: a rodeo term referring to a rule in the bareback and saddle bronc riding disciplines stating the rider must hold both of his feet over the point of the horse's shoulders – with the spur keeping contact with the horse – leaving the bucking chutes and before the horse's front feet hit the ground. Failure to do so is considered "missing the horse out" and results in a no-score.

Mucked Out: a rodeo and cowboy term for when a cowboy or cowgirl takes a really bad hooking from a bull or cow.

NFR: National Finals Rodeo, also referred to as the Wrangler National Finals Rodeo or WNFR, held at the Thomas and Mack Center in Las Vegas, Nevada. This is the premiere event in rodeo. Qualifying to the NFR is one of the most prestigious things a rodeo athlete can accomplish. The Top 15 in the PRCA World Standings, from each discipline, qualify to the NFR. The 10-day, 10-round event determines the NFR Average Champion, based on aggregate score/time over the ten rounds. After all money won from the regular season, each NFR round's placings, and NFR average placings is calculated, the highest money-earner in each discipline is crowned World Champion. The NFR is often referred to as the Super Bowl of Rodeo, because of its prestige and large fanfare. Hundreds of thousands of cowboys, cowgirls, and rodeo fans from all over the world descend on Las Vegas during this time. It is also sometimes referred to as the World Series of Rodeo because it is a Championship event that takes place over multiple days.

No-Score: a rodeo term for a roughstock contestant receiving a score of zero. A no-score is due to bucking off before the 8-second buzzer, failing to mark their horse out on the first jump, or the rider's free hand touching any part of himself, the animal, or his equipment before the buzzer.

No-Time: a rodeo term for a timed event contestant failing to receive a scoreable time in their event. This could be for things like missing their calf or steer in a roping event, breaking their pattern in the barrel racing, etc.

Packed Me Around The Corner: a bull riding term for when a bull rider is in perfect position and is riding a spinning bull with ease. Correct bull riding form puts all of the pressure on the rider's legs. So, when a bull moves in one direction or the other, he pushes up against the rider's legs, the legs move with the bull, and the rider's body follows with the correct motions. When sitting in the pocket, it honestly feels like the bull is taking you around the corner with him, or packing you along for the trip, hence the term "packing me around the corner."

PBR: Professional Bull Riders, Inc. The PBR is one of two majority-recognized professional rodeo organizations. The PRCA (and subsequent NFR) features multiple rodeo disciplines while the PBR specializes in only the bull riding discipline. It was founded by 20 cowboys in 1992 who were disgruntled by the amount of money they felt was being left on the table that bull riders could be making. They were proven right very quickly. Within four years, the PBR grew to a multi-million dollar organization – maintaining that status even today – garnering the highest consistent payouts the sport had ever seen up to that point. The celebrated payout of the few largest PRCA rodeos was equal to what the Bud Light Cup – the highest tier of the PBR at that time, now recognized as the Built Ford Tough Series – was paying *every single weekend*. There is no denying the impact the PBR has had on the amount of money rodeo athletes are able to make today, across all disciplines and organizations.

PBR World Finals: the finals for Professional Bull Riders, Inc. This high-energy event features the best bull riders in the PBR against the best bulls in the world. When I was riding, it was held at MGM Grand in Las Vegas, Nevada. It is now being held at AT&T Stadium, home of the Dallas Cowboys, in Arlington, Texas. The PBR World Champion is crowned at the conclusion of this event. The PBR has been paying a $1 million bonus to their World Champion every year since 2003.

Pen (ranching): a ranching term for a smaller fenced-in area to hold livestock. If a rancher is "penning cows," it means they are gathering them from the pasture and pushing them into a smaller pen, usually one back at ranch headquarters.

Pen (rodeo): a rodeo term referring to the set of animals in the draw for that rodeo or performance. "*The bull you drew is probably the best one in the pen.*" It also refers to a stock contractor's set of animals. "*J Bar J has an outstanding pen of bucking horses*". At the NFR, since it is ten rounds over ten nights, there are specific pens for each performance to keep the draw as even as possible amongst the fifteen contestants. The bucking stock qualify to the NFR just like the athletes do. Making the NFR is just as much a badge of honor to that horse or bull as it is to that contestant. Every animal will buck twice at the NFR, which also means each pen is featured twice. For example, the "Rank Pen" features the best of the best, the rankest bucking bulls and horses on the planet. The "Eliminator Pen" features bulls or horses with a lot of dirty tricks in their arsenal. The "Money Pen" features horses or bulls that are extremely fun to ride, but also have a history of riders scoring high points on them.

Performance/Perf: a rodeo term for each specific showing of a rodeo event in front of a live audience. If a rodeo has 100 contestants performing in each discipline, rather than attempting to have all of them perform in one night, the rodeo committee will spread them out over multiple evenings. Keeping each performance's roster down to 10-15 contestants, in each discipline, allows for the rodeo to stay entertaining for the fans in attendance by not dragging the night out too long. If the rodeo has more contestants competing than performances allow, numerous contestants will compete in what is called "slack." This is usually held in the morning without the normal lights, entertainment, and production a performance provides for fans. The sole purpose of "slack," is to have a large portion of the contestants entered in the event receive a time, or score, while keeping the performance rosters lower for time's sake. The time, or score, made during "slack" counts the same as if the contestant had performed in a performance.

Permit: a rodeo term for what any aspiring professional rodeo athlete, in both the PRCA and PBR, must purchase before they can fulfill that dream. Anyone can buy a permit for a chance to enter professional rodeos, but a certain amount of money must be won on your permit to be able to purchase your card and be considered a professional athlete in that organization. This is called "filling your card." Most rodeos have designated entries set aside for permit-holders to have a chance to fill their card. Once the designated amount of money has been won, the athlete can choose to purchase his card immediately or continue competing on their permit the rest of that year, and purchase their card the following year. Unless they fill their permit early in the season, most contestants choose to remain on their permit so they can give a full year's attempt at the Rookie of the Year title in their discipline the following year. Staying on their permit also allows them to qualify for the Permit Holder of the Year Challenge in Las Vegas, Nevada, held during the NFR.

Pickup Man: a rodeo term for the cowboys on horseback to aid the contestants during the bareback and saddle bronc riding disciplines. After the 8-second buzzer, a pickup man rides along the bucking horse so the bareback rider or bronc rider can dismount off their bucking horse, onto the pickup man's horse, then onto the ground for a safer dismount. The pickup man is also responsible for unclasping the flank strap and back cinch on a bronc saddle before escorting the bucking horse out of the arena. Pickup men are some of the best "horsemen" in all of the sport of rodeo. A pickup man's title is not to be confused with the guys standing around the beer tent after a rodeo. Their title is "buckle bunny chaser."

Pocket: a rodeo term referring to the "sweet spot" on an animal in the roughstock events. The pocket is essentially the perfect position where the rider is in the most control. In bull riding, this is up, over your riding hand – you actually don't want to sit down on a bull's back but rather be riding "up" on your legs with a gap between the bull's back and your butt – with your shoulders and hips lined up perfectly square with the bull's shoulders. When in the pocket, the rider feels less of the animal's power and can use the bull's movement against his legs to anticipate the bull's next move. When outside of the pocket, a rider feels *all* of the bulls power, and the bull can use the rider's momentum to buck him off or jerk him down.

Practice Pen: a rodeo term for when rodeo athletes practice their discipline on a live animal. It is usually a group of cowboys practicing together, but many times it can also be an individual practicing on his own. While hundreds of hours are spent honing muscle memory on a stationary barrel, spur board, or roping dummy, nothing compares to practicing on an actual live animal.

PRCA: Professional Rodeo Cowboys Association. The PRCA is one of two majority-recognized professional rodeo organizations. The PBR specializes in only the bull riding discipline while the PRCA features multiple rodeo disciplines. The year-end finals for the PRCA is called the NFR, and is considered the most prestigious event in all of rodeo. The PRCA was founded in 1936 after a group of cowboys staged a walk-out of a Boston rodeo event, protesting their entry fees not being added to the total purse. It was originally known as the Cowboys' Turtle Association, before changing its name to Rodeo Cowboys Association in 1945, and then to what we know it as today, Professional Rodeo Cowboys Association, in 1975.

Pulling a Rope/Pulled My Rope: a rodeo term for the process of tightening a bull rider's rope around the bull. A helper pulls up on the tail of the bull rope, which tightens it around the bull's body while also squeezing the bull rope's handle tighter on the rider's riding hand. The rider then "takes a wrap," which is the process of laying the rope across the handle/hand, around the back of their hand, and then back over the handle/hand, helping lock the rope in place.

Pulled My Foot: a rodeo term for when a bull rider begins to spur a bull.

Qualified Ride: a rodeo term for when a roughstock rider covers – stays on – their animal for the full 8-seconds and receives a score.

Rank: refers to a bull or horse who bucks very hard. Calling a bucking bull or horse 'rank' is a high compliment. Also if a bull or horse had a really good trip, it can be referred to as a "rank trip". "*Did you see Bootlicker in Chadron last weekend? That was one rank trip for sure!*" If a rider has a really good ride, it can also be referred to as a "rank ride." Pretty much anytime the word "rank" is used in the rodeo world, it's a good thing, unless it's towards your traveling partner a few hours down the road after eating Taco Bell.

Re-Ride: a rodeo term for when a roughstock contestant essentially gets a "do-over" with a new animal. This could be because the rider was fouled leaving the chute, or the judges felt the horse/bull didn't perform as well as the other horses/bulls in the competition. The re-ride horses and bulls are drawn at the beginning of the rodeo as well, so the contestants know which horse/bull they will be getting on if they elect to accept the re-ride.

Riding Hand/Riding Arm: the hand a roughstock rider holds on with, whether it is a bull rope, bareback rigging, or bronc rein.

Riding Percentage: a rodeo term for monitoring a bull rider's buck-offs and rides throughout a season. Similar to a batting average in baseball, riding percentage is a good monitor for how well a rider has been performing all season. Riding percentage is simply how many bulls the rider covered for the full 8-seconds divided by how many bulls the rider got on. It doesn't take into effect how rank the bulls were, simply how often the rider has covered their bulls that season.

Riggin: *see Bareback Rigging*

Rodeo Disciplines: the different sports within the sport of rodeo (i.e. bareback riding, bull riding, team roping, etc.). These are also referred to as rodeo events, but to lessen the confusion with another term for rodeo events, I will continue referring to them as disciplines in this book.

Rodeo Event: a term for an event featuring any rodeo disciplines. Rodeo, as a sport, dates all the way back to the Wild West days, when cowboys from neighboring ranches would devise different competitions to determine who had the handiest cowboys working amongst them. The first recorded rodeo contest was held in Deer Trail, Colorado, in 1864. The first "major organized rodeo event" was put together by Buffalo Bill Cody in North Platte, Nebraska, in 1882. The first "public contest" rodeo event is believed to have been held in Pecos, Texas, in 1883.

Rodeo Secretary: the heartbeat behind any rodeo production. The rodeo secretary is responsible for entries, payouts, draw sheets, check-ins, breaking up fights … You name it! If it involves any aspect of producing the rodeo on hand, then the rodeo secretary probably does it, while somebody else takes the credit for it.

Rodeo Timer: a rodeo term for the person responsible with recording the official time for the timed events and starting the 8-second timer for the roughstock events.

Roping Box: a rodeo term for the area from which a rodeo athlete and their horse leave at the start of any roping disciplines. If the contestant leaves this area too early – *see barrier* – they are assessed a 10-second penalty.

Roping Chute: a rodeo term for the chute a steer or calf leaves for the start of any roping disciplines.

Roping Dummy: a rodeo term for a practice dummy used by rodeo athletes in any roping disciplines. Calf ropers and team ropers spend countless hours standing behind a roping dummy, roping the head of the dummy over and over again, to hone their muscle memory.

Roping Horse: a horse ridden by a rodeo athlete in any of the timed event disciplines. These animals are trained specifically for these events. The best roping horses are sometimes ridden by multiple contestants at the same event.

Roughstock Events/Roughies: the rodeo disciplines that receive a score for their performance: bareback riding, saddle bronc riding, and bull riding. Athletes who compete in these disciplines are considered roughstock cowboys, or roughies. Since roughies are the "wild childs" of rodeo, bull fighters are also thrown into this category. There is a mutual respect, but also a friendly rivalry, between roughies and timeys. Everyone knows that roughies are the tougher, far cooler grouping of the two. My timey friends may disagree. But hey, it's my book so I can persuade the reading audience how I choose.

Saddle Bronc Riders: rodeo athletes who compete in the saddle bronc riding discipline. Also referred to as "bronc riders." These guys are usually very handy around a ranch as well. To me, bronc riders are the most "true cowboy" of all rodeo athletes. Good luck getting a saddle bronc rider to say more than ten sentences in one conversation; unless, of course, that saddle bronc rider throws a wig on his head and becomes a social media influencer as "the world's greatest bull rider."

Saddle Bronc Riding: a rodeo discipline where the athlete rides a bucking horse with a spurring motion that goes from above the horse's shoulders, across the horse's side, behind the rider's torso to the canal of the saddle, and back to above the horse's shoulders. Saddle bronc riding is the most traditional discipline in the entire sport of rodeo and the most poetically beautiful to watch, in my opinion. The rider hangs onto a bronc rein that is attached to a halter on the horse's head and sits in a bronc saddle, specifically designed for this discipline. The rider must stay on for 8-seconds and is then given a score based on the performance of the horse and rider. *To see how a score is calculated, refer to "Score".*

Saddle Bronc Saddle: a saddle used for the saddle bronc riding discipline – also known as a "bronc saddle." It is different from a traditional saddle in that it has no saddle horn, wider swells for the rider to squeeze their legs under, and the stirrups are naturally pointed forward out of the front of the saddle, as opposed to the traditional straight-down stirrups. The saddle is similar to a traditional saddle in that it is secured to the horse via a front and back cinch. A bronc saddle is specifically tailored for each rider, so that when they perform the spurring motion – *see Saddle Bronc Riding* – leather binds in the stirrups perfectly squeeze their legs tighter to the swells. Too tight of binds will force the rider's legs over the swells bucking them off. Too loose of binds will not hold the rider's legs tight enough against the swells, making it impossible to stay on a bucking horse.

Saddle Horse: a cowboy term for a horse trained to be ridden safely. On stock contractor ranches the term "saddle horse" refers to the horses used to ride around the ranch as opposed to their bucking horses.

Score: what is given to contestants in the roughstock events who rode their horse/bull for the full 8-seconds and used to determine where that rider places among his competitors. The highest possible score is 100 points. Judges on each side of the arena give a score based on the performance of the horse/bull and rider from their perspective and vantage point. 1-25 points are awarded the animal for how hard they bucked, and 1-25 points are awarded the rider for how in control they were on the animal, as well as their spurring motion in the horse events; which means each judge gives a score up to 50 points total for the ride. If there are two judges at the event, the two scores are added together to give the final score. If there are four judges, then the four scores are added together and divided by two to give the final score. If there are six judges, typically the highest and lowest scores are dropped, the other four scores added together, and divided by two to give the final score. A score in the high 70s is considered good, low-to-mid 80s great, high 80s outstanding, and anything in the 90s exceptional. The riders are placed by their score, with the winner being the rider with the highest number of points.

Secretary: *see Rodeo Secretary*

Section: a rodeo term for when an athlete competes (i.e., 1st section, 2nd section, etc.) if their discipline is split into multiple groupings that performance.

Short Go-Round/Short Go/Short Round: a rodeo term for what is usually the final round in a multi-round formatted rodeo event. After everyone competes in at least one long go-round, the contestants with the best scores/times – or averages, if more than one round – move on to the short go-round. A short go size is determined before the rodeo, and usually consists of ten or fifteen contestants. Some of the bigger paying rodeos (i.e. Rodeo Houston or Calgary Stampede) have what's called a "Money Round" *after* the short go, consisting of either three or four contestants. The three or four with the best scores/times in the short go move on to a "winner take all" ride-off for that rodeo's championship and large prize money that accompanies it – $50,000 to $100,000, or even a possible million dollars at a rodeo event called The American.

Soggy: a term of endearment towards the talent of a rodeo athlete. Saying someone is "*soggy*" is saying they are extremely talented and hard to beat.

Spotter: a rodeo term for a helper in the roughstock events making sure the rider doesn't get hurt if the horse/bull flips over or jumps while in the chute.

Spur: what a cowboy wears on their boots to urge a horse forwards. The rowels on the end are smooth and do no harm to the animal. In the bull riding discipline, a spur's rowels are locked into place and designed to "bunch" the bull's hide to aid the rider in keeping their feet in contact with the bull's side. The design of spurs and rowels are highly regulated to assure not even the slightest of harm comes to the animals.

Spur Board: a device used to help bareback riders and saddle bronc riders train their muscle memory for their spurring motion. It is usually made of wood, with plywood sides so the rider has a long flat surface to spur on. Their riggin' or saddle straps to the board and the rider practices the spurring motion for hours on end. It is the rodeo equivalent of a tee-ball stand for baseball training.

Spur Hung: a rodeo term for when a rider's spur gets caught in the side or tail of their rope.

Stallion: A male horse that has not been castrated.

Stationary Barrel: a device used to help bull riders train their body's muscle memory. It is usually a barrel, standing off the ground, welded to four legs to keep it in place. It is different from a Mighty-Bucky-style training device, which replicates the up and down motion of a bucking bull. A stationary barrel doesn't move and helps the rider strengthen their groin muscles while also replicating recovering from out of position. It trains muscle memory to automatically make those moves if found in that position on a live bull. I spent hundreds, if not thousands, of hours on the stationary barrel my dad made for me as a child and continued to use it all the way up until my career-ending injury.

Steer: A male bovine that has been castarated. Ranchers only keep a certain number of male bovines as bulls for breeding purposes. All other males are castarated, as the lowered testosterone/hormone levels result in meat that is less tough and has a more desirable flavor profile for consumers. Most males are steered as young calves during branding season, which results in one of the best-tasting cowboy treats: Rocky Mountain oysters. The most popular way to serve Rocky Mountain oysters is breaded and fried at a later time. My personal favorite is serving them fresh, right out of the calf, washed off and cooked immediately on the branding iron fire.

Steer Wrestling: also known as "bull dogging". A rodeo discipline where the contestant jumps from the back of their horse, grabbing the horns of a steer, and wrestling that steer to the ground. The contestant is timed from the moment the steer leaves the roping chute until all four legs of the steer are sideways, after the steer wrestler "dogged", or wrestled him.

Steer Wrestler: also known as "bull dogger." A rodeo athlete who competes in the steer wrestling discipline. They are the "linebackers" of the rodeo world. Big, burly men who are half roughie and half timey. If I ever see a fight break out after a rodeo, I'm taking the side that has the most steer wrestlers on it.

Sticky: a term of endearment describing the talent of a rodeo athlete in the roughstock events. Saying someone is "*sticky*" is saying they are very hard to buck off.

Stock Contractor: a rodeo term for who provides the livestock for a rodeo: horses for the bareback and bronc riding, bulls for the bull riding, and steers or calves for the roping events. Stock contracting is usually a family business, with many of the leading professional rodeo contractor companies handed down through generations. The bloodlines of the multiple generations of their horses and bulls are highly sought after as well. These animals are just as much a part of their family as their kids and grandkids.

Stud: a stallion that is being used for breeding. *Also see Bull Fighters*

Taking a Hooking: *refer to Hooked On*

Taking a Wrap: *see pull a rope*

Tapped Off: a rodeo term for when a roughstock rider gets into a "groove," and falls into perfect timing with their animal.

Timed Events/Timeys: the rodeo disciplines that receive a time for their performance: calf roping, steer wrestling, team roping, etc. Athletes who compete in these disciplines are considered timed event cowboys, or timeys.

Timed Event Championships: a non-sanctioned rodeo competition featuring the best timed event athletes in the world. The Cinch Timed Event Championship of the World was founded in 1985 and is held annually at the Lazy-E Arena in Guthrie, Oklahoma. A contestant must compete in all five timed event disciplines: team roping as a header, team roping as a heeler, steer wrestling, calf roping, and steer roping. Five rounds in each discipline, over three days, crowns the winner, and $100,000 prize, to the athlete with the lowest aggregate time on all twenty-five runs. While it is non-sanctioned as a professional rodeo, this event is considered one of the most prestigious competitions a timey can win.

Timer: *see Rodeo Timer*

Team Roper: rodeo athletes who compete in the team roping discipline. This can be referring to either the header or the heeler. Many team ropers can both head and heel, but most focus on one area when it comes to competing professionally. Speaking of which, I heard Jesus was a team roper back in his day. One of the best, as legend tells it. He was apparently a pretty soggy heeler……Dad jokes in a glossary section?......I'm a dad…..I can't help myself.

Team Roping: the only "team" discipline in all of professional rodeo. A header ropes the horns of a steer, turns him at least 90 degrees, and the heeler ropes the two hind feet of the steer. The team is administered a time from when the steer leaves the roping chute until both the header and heeler have caught the steer and are facing their horses directly at each other with no slack between their ropes and the steer. A 5-second penalty is assessed if only one hind foot is caught.

Traveling Partner: a rodeo term for who rodeo athletes choose to travel up and down the road with.

Trip: refers to each individual performance of an animal. If someone says, "*That bull had a really good trip,*" they are saying that the bull performed really well on that day. If they say, "*Man, he was way more welly that trip,*" they are meaning the bull had a tendency to want to pull the rider to the inside of the spin more than he usually does. What sets rodeo apart from other sports is the unpredictability. Whereas other sports, you can study your opponent and have a good anticipation of what they will do, in rodeo that animal underneath you is highly unpredictable. You can learn the *tendencies* of that animal, but there is no guarantee that is what he will do the trip you are on him. If you expect a bull to spin left, because that's what he always does, the bull will feel your body shifting your weight that direction and may spin to the right instead.

Turned Back: a rodeo term for a bull spinning. If a bull turned back into your hand, then he spun in the direction of your riding hand. If he turned back away from your hand, then he spun in the direction of your free hand, away from your riding hand. If he turned back both ways, then he spun one direction and changed to the other direction during the 8-second duration of the ride.

Turn Out: a rodeo term for withdrawing from a rodeo competition. Stock contractors are paid "per out," or for every animal that leaves the chute. In older days, if a contestant withdrew from the rodeo, their animal was physically turned out of the chute without a rider. The terms "turn out," or "turned my bull/horse out," have now become the industry-wide term used to signify withdrawing from the competition. Many professional athletes will enter multiple rodeos on the same day. Then, depending on what they drew, they choose which rodeos to compete at, mapping their traveling accordingly, and turn out of the others. Contestants have to pay a fine for each event they turn out of.

Vest: *see Protective Vest*

Well/Welly: *see Dropped In The Well*

Whistle: *see Buzzer*

Woofy: a compliment reserved for only the best rodeo athletes in the world. This is a step up from "*sticky*" or "*soggy.*" If one cowboy says that another cowboy "*has some woof in him*" or that "*he's woofy,*" that's a cowboy recognizing that this athlete has all the makings to be one of the Top 15 in the World at his/her discipline.

Yard-Darted: a rodeo term for getting bucked off and slammed hard into the ground during the process.

Acknowledgments

First and foremost, I want to thank my wife, Ivy. I truly would not be able to do life without you. You are my rock, my everything. I *love* getting to do life with you. I wouldn't have been able to push through our many adversities had you not been willing to put your head down with me and keep pushing forward together.

To my kids, Tyler and Gracie. You two make me so proud to be called your father. You have been so patient and supportive through all of my brain issues. You've never complained and have always been there whenever I needed you. You two truly are the best kids any dad could ask for. I can't wait to watch your lives unfold as adults.

To my dad, Dave. You may be my dad, but you have also always been my pastor. Your guidance and wisdom have shaped me into the man I am today. I strive every day to be even half the man that the legendary "Quigley" is.

To my mom in heaven, Cathy. I have never met another person on this earth who has the heart for people like you have. You taught me to always look for the best in people, even if they don't deserve it. Your legacy lives on in your grandchildren, and you would be *so* proud of all three!

To my brother, Nate. My inspiration. My best friend. I hope you know the impact your resilience has had on my life. I love it whenever people connect the dots that you are my brother. I'll always be proud to be known as "Nate's brother".

To my sister, Tammy. I'm so proud of the woman you have become and the amazing family you have. I hate that the age gap between us meant you weren't a part of many of the stories within this book. That doesn't diminish at all the impact you have had on my life. Thank you for stepping in when Mom died. That means more than you will ever know.

To my in-laws, Dick and Denise. I'm so blessed to have the support you two always show. You made an amazing daughter and adopted me immediately into your family as one of your own. It's not lost on me how rare it is to have the great relationship that we have.

To my brother-in-law, Zeb. The *stud.* One of the most humble and honorable men I know. I brag on you every chance I get since you won't brag on yourself. Your military and medical careers have been amazing to watch. Thank you for your 20 years of service to our country, and your service now in Emergency Rooms. Also, thank you for not giving me more concussions for dating your sister. Most men I was confident I could take; you aren't one of them.

To Teresa Underdown, literally the most interesting woman in the world. I could sit and listen to you telling stories of "the good ole days" with RCR and Dale Earnhardt all day. But even more is your guidance and wisdom you have given me over the years. You have forgotten more about the business and PR side of things than most learn in a lifetime, as evidenced by your lasting impact on both NASCAR and the PBR. Thank you for *always* taking my phone call and *always* being willing to instil your wisdom, no matter how ridiculous my question may be.

To Heath Ford, my lifelong friend and "concussion buddy." Thank you for being there when I needed you most and for always being in my corner.

To Cody Custer. The World Champ. The Hall of Famer. My mentor, my coach, my traveling partner, and my friend. You've worn many hats for me throughout the years, and your impact on my life is reflected by all of them. Your influence on the sport of rodeo is generational.

To Bob Smiley, my comedy mentor and friend. The "Cody Custer of the Christian Comedy World." The best compliment I can give. Thank you for believing in me and continuing to always guide me!

To Russ Merck. Thank you for believing in me as a Keynote Speaker and pushing me beyond any boundaries I ever thought possible.

To Karen Harris. Thank you for taking this book journey with me. Your knowledge, guidance, and editing skills have been invaluable.

About the Author

Nick Morrison is a motivational speaker and stand-up comedian currently living in the Houston, Texas, area. He was born in Gillette, Wyoming, and grew up on the Pine Ridge Indian Reservation in South Dakota. He spent the majority of his childhood ranching, training horses with his dad, and riding bucking bulls in the sport of rodeo.

In 1997, at the age of 15, Nick led the church service at a Little Britches Rodeo in Wall, South Dakota. Little did he know this would launch over 25 years of public speaking through many different avenues. He continued to speak regularly at rodeo church services across seven surrounding states throughout his high school rodeo career.

In 1999, Nick was voted in by his peers from across the country as a National Youth Board Officer for the National Little Britches Rodeo Association (NLBRA). During his two-year tenure on the Board he wrote for their members' magazine. Not only did he write a monthly article addressing the members from a Youth Board Officer, but he also wrote a monthly article showcasing different NLBRA members from all over the country who had overcome insurmountable odds or adversity.

That same year, he founded Bull Riders For Christ (BRFC) along with his brother, Nate Morrison, and fellow bull rider, Tim Stuen. BRFC led church services at rodeos all over the country, with their main focus being on mentoring and discipling bull riders of all ages and talent levels. Nick, Nate, Tim, Dustin Luper, Jason Hunsaker, Jason Stuen, and Wiley Petersen became the core group of BRFC. From 1999-2004, Nick contributed consistently as a writer for "The International Harvester," BRFC's inspirational newsletter that was mailed to homes all over the United States.

In 2003, Nick joined PBR Outreach led by Todd Pierce, a ministry that put on bible studies for the professional bull riders and church services for the fans attending PBR events each weekend. Nick helped lead worship at the church services on Sunday mornings while leading bible studies with his fellow bull riders on Saturday nights.

Nick rode bulls collegiately for National American University while also riding professionally on the PBR Tour from 2001-2004. In 2004, at just 21 years old, Nick suffered a career-ending injury and left the rodeo world completely.

Nick took a job in Montgomery, Texas, in 2005 as the Worship Pastor and Youth Pastor at Lone Star Cowboy

Church (LSCC) under the leadership of Randy Weaver. While there, the church grew from around a hundred people meeting in a tent to thousands attending weekly. Their youth ministry grew from around a dozen teenagers to hundreds attending weekly as well.

While speaking at a large Minister's Conference in Minneapolis, Minnesota, in 2009, Nick, on a whim, brought up the possibility of supplying youth ministry to rural churches that can't afford to pay youth pastors but have a prime opportunity to offer rural students a dynamic place to go. More than 20 pastors who were attending the conference showed their interest and Crossfire Ministries was born. Five business owners attending LSCC bought into the vision as well, and fully funded the ministry expenses so that it could be completely free for the rural churches. The focal point of the ministry was to not only supply the churches with high-energy youth services via DVD, but also mentor and train their youth leaders over a two-year period to transition into that role and eventually lead their ministries themselves. At its peak, Crossfire Ministries was supplying youth services and mentoring leaders at 32 locations across twelve states.

Nick stepped down from his role at LSCC in 2012 and took an executive position, Director of Ministries, at Dayton Christian Center (DCC) in Dayton, Texas, under the leadership of David Hilton. His role there is to oversee all of the logistics and leadership of every ministry within the church. He led DCC's youth ministry as well during his first few years there. He brought Crossfire Ministries with him to DCC, but transitioned it fully to a mentoring role. The ministry's new focus was on developing the leaders within the youth groups they had been supplying youth ministry to until they were fully self-sustainable. While Crossfire Ministries is no longer active, Nick maintains his role as Director of Ministries at DCC to this day.

Nick began pursuing standup comedy in 2019, with it gaining a lot of traction in 2021. He has traveled all over the United States with other great comedians, including Bob Smiley, Chad Prather, Jaron Myers, Mark Paul, and many more. This career is still in what is considered its "infancy," so it will be exciting to watch it develop even more in the future.

Motivational and inspirational speaking have always been a part of Nick's life. Through most of his life, Nick only pursued these speaking engagements when the opportunity presented itself. With each development you will read about in this book, Nick progressively pursued speaking opportunities more aggressively. In 2023, it became his main focus. He has recently signed with multiple speaking bureaus internationally and is now pursuing motivational and inspirational speaking full time.

To know Nick is to know that he truly has a heart for other people. Compassion drives every project, career, or decision he makes; always trying to find the next way to make an impact on somebody else's life.

Follow Nick on Social Media:
Instagram: @NickMorrisonComedy
Facebook: @PNickM
Facebook: @NickMorrisonComedy

Join the Mailing List at *www.NickMorrisonComedy.com* to have early access to tickets and stay up to date with everything Nick Morrison related.

Made in the USA
Coppell, TX
22 February 2026

72087380R00204